Abraham Cowley

Select Works of Mr. A. Cowley

Vol. I

Abraham Cowley

Select Works of Mr. A. Cowley
Vol. I

ISBN/EAN: 9783337176952

Printed in Europe, USA, Canada, Australia, Japan

Cover: Foto ©ninafisch / pixelio.de

More available books at **www.hansebooks.com**

SELECT WORKS,

IN

VERSE AND PROSE,

OF

MR. A. COWLEY.

VOL. I.

SELECT WORKS
OF MR. A. COWLEY;
IN TWO VOLUMES:
With a PREFACE and NOTES by the Editor.
VOLUME THE FIRST.

Drawn & engrav'd by John Hall, from an Original Picture painted by Zinck in Enamel, in the Collection of the Hon.ble Horace Walpole.

THE THIRD EDITION.

" Forgot his Epic, nay Pindaric art ;
" But ftill we love the language of his heart." POPE.

LONDON:
Printed for T. CADELL, IN THE STRAND.
MDCCLXXVII.

PREFACE.

IT would be uſing moſt writers of name very ill, to treat them with that freedom, which I have preſumed to take with Mr. Cowley. But every thing he wrote, is either ſo good or ſo bad, that, in all reaſon, a ſeparation ſhould be made; leſt the latter, which unhappily, is the greater part, ſhould, in the end, ſtifle and overlay the former.

THE reaſon of this ſtriking difference in the compoſitions of the ſame man, whoſe genius and learn-

ing

ing are unqueſtionable, is, That he
generally followed the taſte of his
time, which was the worſt imaginable ; and rarely his own, which
was naturally excellent; as may be
ſeen in the few pieces of his poetry,
here ſelected from the reſt ; and,
eſpecially, in his proſe-works, which
(except the notes on his *Pindaric
Odes,* and *Davideis*) are given entire,
and have no common merit.

But the talents, by which he is
diſtinguiſhed, as a polite writer,
are the leaſt of his praiſe. There
is ſomething in him, which pleaſes
above his wit, and in ſpite of it.
It is that moral air, and tender ſen-
ſibility of mind, which every one
perceives and loves in reading Mr.
Cowley.

Cowley. And this character of his genius, though it be expressed, indeed, in his other writings, comes out especially, and takes our attention most, in some of his *smaller poems and essays*; which, therefore, it seemed to be for the author's credit, and the convenience of his readers, to draw near to each other, and place, together, in one view. I have said—*for the convenience of his readers:* for, though all are capable of being entertained, perhaps instructed, by the image of a good mind, when set before them, yet few will be at the pains to seek that instruction or entertainment for themselves, through the scattered works of so unequal and voluminous a writer.

To

To do juſtice to the memory of Mr. Cowley, in theſe two reſpects, I mean, in his capacity both of a polite and moral writer, is the ſole end of this publication. Every man of taſte and virtue will read it with pleaſure. There are, indeed, many lines diſperſed through his other poems, which deſerve praiſe. But, on the whole, it is enough if this ſmall collection go down to poſterity : In that caſe, neither they, nor the author, will have any great loſs, though the reſt be forgotten.

Lincoln's-Inn,
April 21, 1772.

R. HURD.

C O N-

�✖✖✖✖✖✖✖✖✖✖✖✖✖✖✖✖✖✖✖✖✖✖

CONTENTS

OF

VOLUME the FIRST.

POEMS.

b   VI. On

CONTENTS.

AN

AN ACCOUNT

OF

The LIFE and WRITINGS

Of Mr. ABRAHAM COWLEY.

Written to Mr. CLIFFORD:

Prefixed to the Folio Edition of 1668.

S I R,

MR. COWLEY in his will recommended to my care the revifing of all
his works that were formerly printed, and
the collecting of thofe papers which he had
defigned for the prefs. And he did it
with this particular obligation, *That I
fhould be fure to let nothing pafs, that
might feem the leaft offence to religion or*

VOL. I.   B   *good*

good manners. A caution, which you will judge to have been altogether needlefs. For certainly, in all ancient or modern times, there can fcarce any author be found, that has handled fo many different matters in fuch various forts of ftyle, who lefs wants the correction of his friends, or has lefs reafon to fear the feverity of ftrangers.

ACCORDING to his defire and his own intention, I have now fet forth his Latin and Englifh writings, each in a volume apart ; and to that which was before extant in both languages, I have added all that I could find in his clofet, which he had brought to any manner of perfection. I have thus, Sir, performed the will of the dead. . But I doubt I fhall not fatisfy the expectation of the living, unlefs fome account be here premifed concerning this excellent man. I know very well, that he has given the world the beft image of his own mind in thefe immortal monuments of his Wit.

Yet

Yet there is ftill room enough left, for one of his familiar acquaintance to fay many things of his poems, and chiefly of his life, that may ferve for the information of his readers, if not for the increafe of his name; which, without any fuch helps, is already fufficiently eftablifhed.

THIS, Sir, were an argument moft proper for you to manage, in refpect of your great abilities, and the long friendfhip you maintained with him. But you have an obftinate averfion from publifhing any of your Writings. I guefs what pretence you have for it, and that you are confirmed in this refolution by the prodigious multitude and imperfections of us writers of this age. I will not now difpute, whether you are in the right; though I am confident you would contribute more to our reformation by your example, than reproofs. But however, feeing you perfift in your purpofe, and have refufed to adorn even this very fubject, which you love fo well; I beg your

affiftance

affiftance while I myfelf undertake it. This
I do with the greater willingnefs, becaufe
I believe there is no man, who fpeaks of
Mr. COWLEY, that can want either matter
or words.   I only therefore intreat you to
give me leave to make you a party in this
relation, by ufing your name and your
teftimony. For by this means, though the
memory of our friend fhall not be delivered to pofterity with the advantage of your
wit, which were moft to be defired ; yet
his praife will be ftrengthened by the confent of your judgement, and the authority
of your approbation.

MR. A. COWLEY was born in the city of
London, in the year one thoufand fix hundred and eighteen. His parents were citizens of a virtuous life and fufficient eftate ;
and fo the condition of his fortune was
equal to the temper of his mind, which
was always content with moderate things.
The firft years of his youth were fpent in
Weftminfter-fchool, where he foon obtained

ed and increafed the noble genius peculiar
to that place. The occafion of his firft
inclination to poetry, was his cafual light-
ing on SPENSER's *Fairy Queen*, when he
was but juft able to read. That indeed is
a poem fitter for the examination of men,
than the confideration of a child. But in
him it met with a fancy, whofe ftrength
was not to be judged by the number of
his years.

IN the thirteenth year of his age there
came forth a little book under his name,
in which there were many things that
might well become the vigour and force of
a manly wit. The firft beginning of his
ftudies, was a familiarity with the moft folid and unaffected authors of antiquity,
which he fully digefted, not only in his
memory, but his judgement. By this advantage he learnt nothing while a boy, that
he needed to forget or forfake when he
came to be a man. His mind was rightly
feafoned at firft; and he had nothing to do,

but

but ſtill to proceed on the ſame foundation on which he began.

He was wont to relate, that he had this defect in his memory at that time, that his teachers could never bring it to retain the ordinary rules of grammar. However, he ſupplied that want, by converſing with the books themſelves, from whence thoſe rules had been drawn. That, no doubt, was a better way, though much more difficult; and he afterwards found this benefit by it, that, having got the Greek and Roman languages, as he had done his own, not by precept but uſe, he practiſed them, not as a ſcholar but a native.

With theſe extraordinary hopes he was removed to Trinity College in Cambridge; where, by the progreſs and continuance of his wit, it appeared that two things were joined in it, which ſeldom meet together, that it was both early ripe and laſting. This brought him into the love and eſteem
of

of the moſt eminent members of that famous ſociety; and principally of your uncle
Mr. FOTHERBY, whoſe favours he ſince
abundantly acknowledged, when his bene-
factor had quite forgot the obligation. His
exerciſes of all kinds are ſtill remembered
in that univerſity with great applauſe; and
with this particular praiſe, that they were
not only fit for the obſcurity of an acade-
mical life, but to have been ſhown on the
true theatre of the world. There it was
that, before the twentieth year of his age,
he laid the deſign of divers of his moſt
maſculine works, that he finiſhed long after:
in which I know not whether I ſhould moſt
commend, that a mind ſo young ſhould conceive ſuch great things, or that it ſhould
be able to perfect them with ſuch felicity.

THE firſt occaſion of his entering into
buſineſs, was the elegy that he writ on Mr.
HERVEY's death : wherein he deſcribed
the higheſt characters of religion, knowledge, and friendſhip, in an age when moſt
other

other men scarce begin to learn them. This brought him into the acquaintance of Mr. JOHN HERVEY, the brother of his deceased friend ; from whom he received many offices of kindness through the whole course of his life, and principally this, that by his means he came into the service of my lord ST. ALBANS.

WHEN the civil war broke out, his affection to the King's cause drew him to Oxford, as soon as it began to be the chief seat of the Royal party. In that university he prosecuted the same studies with a like success. Nor in the mean time was he wanting to his duty in the war itself, for he was present and in service in several of the King's journies and expeditions. By these occasions and the report of his high deserts, he speedily grew familiar to the chief men of the court and the gown, whom the fortune of the war had drawn together. And particularly, though he was then very young, he had the entire friend-

ship

ſhip of my Lord FALKLAND, one of the
principal ſecretaries of ſtate. That affection was contracted by the agreement
of their learning and manners. For you
may remember, Sir, we have often heard
Mr. COWLEY admire him, not only for the
profoundneſs of his knowledge, which was
applauded by all the world, but more
eſpecially for thoſe qualities which he himſelf more regarded, for his generoſity of
mind, and his neglect of the vain pomp
of human greatneſs.

DURING the heat of the civil war, he
was ſettled in my Lord ST. ALBANS' family, and attended her Majeſty the Queen-
mother, when, by the unjuſt perſecution of
her ſubjects, ſhe was forced to retire into
France. Upon this wandering condition
of the moſt vigorous part of his life, he
was wont to reflect, as the cauſe of the long
interruption of his ſtudies. Yet we have
no reaſon to think that he loſt ſo great a
ſpace of time, if we conſider in what buſineſs

nefs he employed his banifhment. He was
abfent from his native country above
twelve years; which were wholly fpent, either in bearing a fhare in the diftreffes of
the royal family, or in labouring in their
affairs. To this purpofe, he performed feveral dangerous journies, into Jerfey, Scot-
land, Flanders, Holland, or wherever elfe
the King's troubles required his attendance.
But the chief teftimony of his fidelity was,
the laborious fervice he underwent, in maintaining the conftant correfpondence between the late King and the Queen his wife.
In that weighty truft he behaved himfelf
with indefatigable integrity and unfufpected
fecrecy. For he cyphered and decyphered,
with his own hand, the greateft part of all
the letters that paffed between their Ma-
jefties, and managed a vaft intelligence in
many other parts : which for fome years
together took up all his days, and two or
three nights every week.

At length, upon his prefent Majefty's
removal out of France, and the Queen-
mother's

mother's ftaying behind, the bufinefs of
that nature paſſed of courfe into other
hands.   Then it was thought fit, by thofe
on whom he depended, that he fhould come
over into England, and, under pretence of
privacy and retirement, fhould take occafion of giving notice of the pofture of
things in this nation.   Upon his return,
he found his country groaning under the
oppreffion of an unjuſt ufurpation.   And
he foon felt the effects of it.   For, while
he lay hid in London, he was feized on by
a miftake, the fearch having been intended
after another gentleman, of confiderable
note in the King's party.   Being made a
prifoner, he was often examined before the
Ufurpers, who tried all imaginable ways to
make him ferviceable to their ends.   That
courfe not prevailing, he was committed
to a fevere reftraint; and fcarce at laft obtained his liberty upon the hard terms of
a thoufand pound bail, which burden Dr.
SCARBOROUGH very honourably took upon
himfelf.   Under thefe bonds he continued
till

till the general redemption. Yet, taking the opportunity of the confufions that followed upon CROMWELL's death, he ventured back into France; and there remained in the fame ftation as before, till near the time of the King's return.

THIS certainly, Sir, is abundantly fufficient to juftify his loyalty to all the world; though fome have endeavoured to bring it in queftion, upon occafion of a few lines in the Preface to one of his books. The objection I muft not pafs by in filence, becaufe it was the only part of his life that was liable to mifinterpretation, even by the confeffion of thofe that envied his fame. In this cafe perhaps it were enough, to alledge for him to men of moderate minds, that what he there faid was publifhed before a book of poetry, and fo ought rather to be efteemed as a problem of his fancy and invention, than as the real image of his judgement. But his defence in this matter may be laid on a

furer

furer foundation. This is the true reafon that is to be given of his delivering
that opinion. Upon his coming over, he
found the ftate of the Royal party very
defperate. He perceived the ftrength of
their enemies fo united, that, till it fhould
begin to break within itfelf, all endeavours
againft it were like to prove unfuccefsful.
On the other fide, he beheld their zeal for
his Majefty's caufe to be ftill fo active,
that it often hurried them into inevitable
ruin. He faw this with much grief. And
though he approved their conftancy as
much as any man living, yet he found their
unfeafonable fhewing it, did only difable
themfelves, and give their adverfaries great
advantages of riches and ftrength by their
defeats. He therefore believed that it
would be a meritorious fervice to the King,
if any man, who was known to have followed his intereft, could infinuate into the
Ufurpers' minds, that men of his principles
were now willing to be quiet, and could
perfuade the poor oppreffed Royalifts to
conceal

conceal their affections, for better occasions. And as for his own particular, he was a close prisoner when he writ that against which the exception is made ; so that he saw it was impossible for him to pursue the ends for which he came hither, if he did not make some kind of declaration of his peaceable intentions. This was then his opinion. And the success of things seems to prove, that it was not very ill grounded. For certainly it was one of the greatest helps to the King's affairs, about the latter end of that tyranny, that many of his best friends dissembled their counsels, and acted the same designs, under the disguises and names of other parties.

THIS, Sir, you can testify to have been the innocent occasion of these words, on which so much clamour was raised. Yet seeing his good intentions were so ill interpreted, he told me, the last time that ever I saw him, that he would have them omitted in the next impression : of which his

friend

friend Mr. Cook is a witnefs. However, if we fhould take them in the worft fenfe of which they are capable: yet, methinks, for his maintaining one falfe tenet in the political philofophy, he made a fufficient atonement, by a continual fervice of twenty years, by the perpetual loyalty of his dif- courfe, and by many of his other writings, wherein he has largely defended and adorn- ed the Royal caufe. And to fpeak of him, not as our friend, but according to the common laws of humanity; certainly, that life muft needs be very unblameable, which had been tried in bufinefs of the higheft confequence, and practifed in the hazard- ous fecrets of courts and cabinets; and yet there can nothing difgraceful be pro- duced againft it, but only the error of one paragraph, and a fingle metaphor.

But to return to my narration, which this digreffion has interrupted: Upon the King's happy reftoration, Mr. Cowley was paft the fortieth year of his age; of which

which the greateſt part had been ſpent in
a various and tempeſtuous condition. He
now thought he had ſacrificed enough of
his life to his curioſity and experience. He
had enjoyed many excellent occaſions of
obſervation. He had been preſent in many
great revolutions, which in that tumultu-
ous time diſturbed the peace of all our
neighbour-ſtates, as well as our own. He
had nearly beheld all the ſplendour of the
higheſt part of mankind. He had lived
in the preſence of princes, and familiarly
converſed with greatneſs in all its degrees,
which was neceſſary for one that would
contemn it aright: for to ſcorn the pomp
of the world before a man knows it, does
commonly proceed rather from ill-manners than a true magnanimity.

He was now weary of the vexations and
formalities of an active condition. He had
been perplexed with a long compliance to
foreign manners. He was ſatiated with
the arts of court: which ſort of life,
though

though his virtue had made innocent to
him, yet nothing could make it quiet.
Thefe were the reafons that moved him to
forego all public employments, and to
follow the violent inclination of his own
mind, which, in the greateft throng of his
former bufinefs, had ftill called upon him,
and reprefented to him the true delights
of folitary ftudies, of temperate pleafures,
and of a moderate revenue, below the malice and flatteries of fortune.

AT firft he was but flenderly provided
for fuch a retirement, by reafon of his
travels, and the afflictions of the party to
which he adhered, which had put him
quite out of all the roads of gain. Yet,
notwithftanding the narrownefs of his in-
come, he remained fixed to his refolution,
upon his confidence in the temper of his
own mind, which he knew had contracted
its defires into fo fmall a compafs, that a
very few things would fupply them all.
But upon the fettlement of the peace of

our nation, this hinderance of his defign
was foon removed; for he then obtained
a plentiful eftate, by the favour of my Lord
St. Albans, and the bounty of my Lord
Duke of Buckingham; to whom he was
always moft dear, and whom he ever re-
fpected, as his principal patrons. The laft
of which great men, you know, Sir, it is
my duty to mention, not only for Mr.
Cowley's fake, but my own : though I
cannot do it, without being afhamed, that,
having the fame encourager of my ftudies,
I fhould deferve his patronage fo much
lefs.

Thus he was fufficiently furnifhed for
his retreat. And immediately he gave
over all purfuit of honour and riches, in a
time, when, if any ambitious or covetous
thoughts had remained in his mind, he
might juftly have expected to have them
readily fatisfied. In his laft feven or eight
years, he was concealed in his beloved
obfcurity, and poffeffed that folitude, which
                                    from

from his very childhood he had always moft paffionately defired. Though he had frequent invitations to return into bufinefs, yet he never gave ear to any perfuafions of profit or preferment, His vifits to the city and court were very few : his ftays in town were only as a paffenger, not an inhabitant. The places that he chofe for the feats of his declining life, were two or three villages on the bank of the Thames. During this recefs, his mind was rather exercifed on what was to come, than what was paffed ; he fuffered no more bufinefs nor cares of life to come near him, than what were enough to keep his foul awake, but not to difturb it. Some few friends and books, a chearful heart, and innocent confcience, were his conftant companions. His poetry indeed he took with him, but he made that an anchorite as well as himfelf : he only dedicated it to the fervice of his Maker, to defcribe the great images of religion and virtue wherewith his mind abounded. And he employed his mufic

to no other ufe, than as his own DAVID did
.towards SAUL, by finging the praifes of
GOD and of Nature, to drive the evil fpirit
out of men's minds.

OF his works [a] that are publifhed, it is
hard to give one general character, becaufe
of the difference of their fubjects, and the
various forms and diftant times of their
writing. Yet this is true of them all, that
in all the feveral fhapes of his ftyle, there
is ftill very much of the likenefs and impreffion of the fame mind; the fame unaffected modefty, and natural freedom, and
eafy vigour, and chearful paffions, and innocent mirth, which appeared in all his
manners. We have many things that he
writ in two very unlike conditions, in the
univerfity and the court. But in his poe-

[a] *Of his works*] The ill faith of a friend, in
commending every thing alike, and without referve,
would be very confpicuous in all that follows to p. 41,
if we did not reflect, that, what fuch a poet, as Mr.
Cowley, was capable of writing, fuch a critic, as Dr.
Sprat, may be fuppofed very honeftly to approve.

try,

try, as well as his life, he mingled with excellent fkill what was good in both ftates. In his life, he joined the innocence and fincerity of the fcholar with the humanity and good behaviour of the courtier. In his poems, he united the folidity and art of the one with the gentility and gracefulnefs of the other.

If any fhall think that he was not wonderfully curious in the choice and elegance of all his words: I will affirm with more truth on the other fide, that he had no manner of affectation in them; he took them as he found them made to his hands; he neither went before, nor came after, the ufe of the age. He forfook the converfation, but never the language, of the city and court. 'He underftood exceeding well all the variety and power of poetical numbers; and practifed all forts with great happinefs. If his verfes in fome places feem not as foft and flowing as fome would have them, it was his choice, not his fault.

He

He knew that, in diverting men's minds, there fhould be the fame variety obferved as in the profpects of their eyes : where a rock, a precipice, or a rifing wave, is often more delightful, than a fmooth even ground, or a calm fea.   Where the matter required it, he was as gentle as any man. But where higher virtues were chiefly to be regarded, an exact numerofity was not then his main care.   This may ferve to anfwer thofe who upbraid fome of his pieces with roughnefs, and with more contractions than they are willing to allow.   But thefe admirers of gentlenefs without finews, fhould know that different arguments muft have different colours of fpeech: that there is a kind of variety of fexes in poetry, as well as in mankind: that, as the peculiar excellence of the feminine kind is fmoothnefs and beauty ; fo ftrength is the chief praife of the mafculine.

He had a perfect maftery in both the languages in which he writ : but each of
them

them kept a juſt diſtance from the other ;
neither did his Latin make his Engliſh too
old, nor his Engliſh make his Latin too
modern. He excelled both in proſe and
verſe; and both together have that perfection, which is commended by ſome of
the ancients above all others, that they are
very obvious to the conception, but moſt
difficult in the imitation.

His fancy flowed with great ſpeed; and
therefore it was very fortunate to him,
that his judgement was equal to manage it.
He never runs his reader nor his argument out of breath. He perfectly practiſes
the hardeſt ſecret of good writing, to know
when he has done enough. He always
leaves off in ſuch a manner, that it appears
it was in his power to have ſaid much
more. In the particular expreſſions there
is ſtill much to be applauded, but more in
the diſpoſition and order of the whole.
From thence there ſprings a new comeli-
neſs, beſides the feature of each part. His

invention

invention is powerful, and large as can
be defired. But it feems all to arife out
of the nature of the fubject, and to be
juft fitted for the thing of which he fpeaks.
If ever he goes far for it, he diffembles his
pains admirably well.

The variety of arguments that he has
managed is fo large, that there is fcarce
any particular of all the paffions of men,
or works of Nature and Providence, which
he has paffed by undefcribed. Yet he
ftill obferves the rules of decency with fo
much care, that whether he inflames his
reader with the fofter affections, or delights
him with inoffenfive raillery, or teaches
the familiar manners of life, or adorns the
difcoveries of philofophy, or infpires him
with the heroic characters of charity and
religion ; to all thefe matters, that are fo
wide afunder, he ftill proportions a due
figure of fpeech, and a proper meafure of
wit. This indeed is moft remarkable, that
a man who was fo conftant and fixed in
the

the moral ideas of his mind, fhould yet be
fo changeable in his intellectual, and in
both to the higheft degree of excellence.

If there needed any excufe to be made,
that his love-verfes fhould take up fo great
a fhare in his works; it may be alledged,
that they were compofed when he was very
young. But it is a vain thing to make
any kind of apology for that fort of writings. If devout or virtuous men will fu-
percilioufly forbid the minds of the young,
to adorn thofe fubjects about which they
are moft converfant, they would put
them out of all capacity of performing
graver matters, when they come to them.
For the exercifes of all mens wits muft be
always proper for their age, and never too
much above it: and by practice and ufe
in lighter arguments, they grow up at laft
to excel in the moft weighty. I am not
therefore afhamed to commend Mr. Cow-
LEY's Miftrefs. I only except one or two
expreffions, which I wifh I could have prevailed

vailed with thofe that had the right of the other edition, to have left out. But of all the reft I dare boldly pronounce, that never yet fo much was written on a fubject fo delicate, that can lefs offend the fevereft rules of morality. The whole paffion of love is inimitably defcribed, with all its mighty train of hopes, and joys, and dif-quiets. Befides this amorous tendernefs, I know not how, in every copy, there is fomething of more ufeful knowledge very naturally and gracefully infinuated ; and every where there may be fomething found, to inform the minds of wife men as well as to move the hearts of young men or women.

THE occafion of his falling on the Pin-daric way of writing, was his accidental meeting with PINDAR's works, in a place where he had no other books to direct him [b]. Having then confidered at leifure

[b] —direct him] So it ftands in all the editions I have feen. But the proper word feems to be — divert.

the

the height of his invention, and the majefty of his ftyle, he tried immediately to imitate it in Englifh. And he performed it without the danger that Horace prefaged to man who fhould dare to attempt it.

If any are difpleafed at the boldnefs of his metaphors, and length of his digreffion, they contend not againft Mr. Cowley, but Pindar himfelf; who was fo much reverenced by all antiquity, that the place of his birth was preferved as facred, when his native city was twice deftroyed by the fury of two conquerors. If the irregularity of the number difguft them, they may obferve that this very thing makes that kind of poefy fit for all manner of fubjects: for the pleafant, the grave, the amorous, the heroic, the philofophical, the moral, the divine. Befides this, they will find, that the frequent alteration of the rhythm and feet affects the mind with a more various delight, while it is foon apt to be tired by the fettled pace of any

one

one conſtant meaſure. But that for which I think this inequality of number is chiefly to be preferred, is its near affinity with proſe: from which all other kinds of Engliſh verſe are ſo far diſtant, that it is very ſeldom found that the ſame man excels in both ways. But now this looſe and unconfined meaſure has all the grace and harmony of the moſt confined. And withal, it is ſo large and free, that the practice of it will only exalt, not corrupt, our proſe: which is certainly the moſt uſeful kind of writing of all others: for it is the ſtyle of all buſineſs and converſation.

Besides this imitating of Pindar, which may perhaps be thought rather a new ſort of writing, than a reſtoring of an ancient; he has alſo been wonderfully happy, in tranſlating many difficult parts of the nobleſt poets of antiquity. To perform this according to the dignity of the attempt, he had, as it was neceſſary he ſhould have, not only the elegance of both the

the languages, but the true fpirit of both
the poetries. This way of leaving verbal
tranflations, and chiefly regarding the fenfe
and genius of the author, was fcarce heard
of in England, before this prefent age,
I will not prefume to fay, that Mr. Cow-
LEY was the abfolute inventor of it. Nay,
I know that others had the good luck to
recommend it firft in print. Yet I appeal
to you, Sir, whether he did not conceive
it, and difcourfe of it, and practife it, as
foon as any man.

His Davideis was wholly written in fo
young an age; that, if we fhall reflect on
the vaftnefs of the argument, and his manner of handling it, he may feem like one
of the miracles that he there adorns, like
a boy attempting Goliah. I have often
heard you declare, that he had finifhed the
greateft part of it, while he was yet a young
ftudent at Cambridge. This perhaps may
be the reafon, that in fome few places, there
is more youthfulnefs and redundance of
fancy

fancy than his riper judgement would have
allowed. I know, Sir, you will give me
leave to ufe this liberty of cenfure; for I
do not here pretend to a profeffed panegyric, but rather to give a juft opinion concerning him. But for the main of it, I
will affirm, that it is a better inftance and
beginning of a divine poem, than I ever
yet faw in any language. The contrivance
is perfectly ancient, which is certainly the
true form of heroic poetry, and fuch as
was never yet outdone by any new devices
of modern wits. The fubject was truly
divine, even according to God's own heart.
The matter of his invention, all the treafures of knowledge and hiftories in the
Bible. The model of it comprehended
all the learning of the Eaft. The characters, lofty and various: the numbers,
firm and powerful: the digreffions, beautiful and proportionable: the defign, to fub-
mit mortal wit to heavenly truths: in all
there is an admirable mixture of human
virtues and paffions, with religious rap-
·tures.   THE

THE truth is, Sir, methinks, in other matters, his wit excelled moſt other mens : but in his moral and divine works, it out-did itſelf. And no doubt it proceeded from this cauſe; that in other lighter kinds of poetry, he chiefly repreſented the humours and affections of others; but in theſe he ſat to himſelf, and drew the figure of his own mind. I know it has been objected againſt him, by ſome moroſe zealots, that he has done an injury to the Scripture, by ſprinkling all his works with many alluſions and ſimilitudes that he took out of the Bible. But to theſe men it were a ſufficient reply, to compare their own practice with his, in this particular. They make uſe of Scripture phraſes and quotations, in all their common diſcourſe. They employ the words of Holy Writ, to countenance the extravagance of their own opinions and affections. And why then might not he take the liberty to fetch from thence ſome ornament,

ornament, for the innocent paffions, and
natural truths, and moral virtues,. which
he defcribes ?

THIS is confutation enough to that fort
of men. As to the thing itfelf, it is fo far
from being a debafing of divinity, to make
fome parts of it the fubjects of our fancy,
that it is a fure way to eftablifh it familiarly
on the hearts of the people, and to give it
a durable impreffion on the minds of wife
men. Of this we have a powerful inftance amongft the ancients. For their
wit has lafted much longer than the practice of any of their religions. And the
very memory of moft of their divine worfhip had perifhed, if it had not been expreffed and preferved by their poets. But
Mr. COWLEY himfelf did of all men living abhor the abufe of Scripture by licen-
tious raillery; which ought not only to
be efteemed the meaneft kind of wit, but
the worft fort of ill-manners. This perhaps fome men would be loth to hear
                                        proved,

proved, who practife it under the falfe title of a genteel quality : but the truth of it is unqueftionable. For the ordinary ill-breeding is only an indecence and offence againft fome particular cuftom, or gefture, or behaviour in ufe. But this p:bphane-nefs is a violation of the very fupport of human fociety, and a rudenefs againft the beft manners that all mankind can prac-tife, which is, a juft reverence of the Su-preme Power of all the world.

In his Latin poems, he has expreffed to admiration, all the numbers of verfe, and figures of poefy, that are fcattered up and down amongft the ancients. There is hardly to be found in them all any good fafhion of fpeech, or colour of meafure, but he has comprehended it, and given inftances of it, according as his feveral ar-guments required either a majeftic fpirit, or a paffionate, or a pleafant. This is the more extraordinary, in that it was never yet performed by any fingle poet of the ancient Romans themfelves. They had the language natural to them, and fo might eafily have moulded it into what form or humour they pleafed: yet it was their con-ftant cuftom, to confine all their thoughts and practice to one or two ways of writing, as defpairing ever to compafs all together. This is evident, in thofe that excelled in odes and fongs, in the comical, tragical, epical, elegiacal, or fatyrical way. And this perhaps occafioned the firft diftinction and number of the Mufes. For they thought the tafk too hard for any one of them, though they fancied them to be goddeffes. And therefore they divided it among them all; and only recommended to each of them, the care of a diftinct cha-racter of poetry and mufic.

THE occafion of his chufing the fub-ject of his fix books of plants, was this: when he returned into England, he was advifed to diffemble the main intention of his coming over, under the difguife of applying

plying himſelf to ſome ſettled profeſſion.
And that of phyſic was thought moſt proper. To this purpoſe, after many anatomical diſſections, he proceeded to the con-
ſideration of Simples; and having furniſh-
ed himſelf with books of that nature, he
retired into a fruitful part of Kent, where
every field and wood might ſhew him the
real figures of thoſe plants of which he
read. Thus he ſpeedily maſtered that part
of the art of medicine. But then, as one
of the ancients did before him in the ſtudy of
the law, inſtead of employing his ſkill
for practice and profit, he preſently digeſt-
ed it into that form which we behold.

THE two firſt books treat of Herbs, in
a ſtyle reſembling the elegies of Ovid and
Tibullus, in the ſweetneſs and freedom
of the verſe; but excelling them in the
ſtrength of the fancy, and vigour of the
ſenſe. The third and fourth diſcourſe of
Flowers in all the variety of CATULLUS
and HORACE's numbers: for the laſt of
which

which authors he had a peculiar reverence,
and imitated him, not only in the ftately
and numerous pace of his odes and epodes,
but in the familiar eafinefs of his epiftles
and fpeeches. The two laft fpeak of Trees,
in the way of Virgil's Georgics. Of
thefe the fixth book is wholly dedicated
to the honour of his country. For, making
the Britifh Oak to prefide in the affembly
of the foreft trees, upon that occafion he
enlarges on the hiftory of our late troubles,
the King's affliction and return, and the
beginning of the Dutch war: and mana-
ges all in a ftyle, that (to fay all in a
word) is equal to the greatnefs and valour
of the Englifh nation.

I told you, Sir, that he was very happy in the way of Horace's fpeeches.
But of this there are but two inftances
preferved: that part of an epiftle to Mr.
Creswel, with which he concludes his
preface to his book of plants: and that
copy which is written to yourfelf. I confefs,

fefs, I heartily wifh he had left more examples behind him of this kind : becaufe
I efteem it to be one of the beft and moft
difficult, of all thofe that antiquity has
taught us.　It is certainly the very original of true raillery ; and differs as much
from fome of the other Latin fatyrs, as the
pleafant reproofs of a gentleman, from the
feverity of a fchool-mafter.　I know fome
men difapprove it, becaufe the verfe feems
to be loofe, and near to the plainnefs of
common difcourfe.　But that which was
admired by the court of Auguftus, never
ought to be efteemed flat, or vulgar.　And
the fame judgement fhould be made of
mens ftyles, as of their behaviour and car-
riage : wherein that is moft courtly, and
hardeft to be imitated, which confifts of a
natural eafinefs and unaffected grace, where
nothing feems to be ftudied, yet every
thing is extraordinary.

THIS familiar way of verfe puts me in
mind of one kind of profe wherein Mr.

COWLEY was excellent; and that is, his letters to his private friends. In thefe he
always exprefled the native tendernefs and
innocent gaiety of his mind. I think, Sir,
you and I have the greateft collection of
this fort. But I know you agree with me,
that nothing of this nature fhould be publifhed: and herein you have always con-
fented to approve of the modeft judgement
of our countrymen, above the practice of
fome of our neighbours, and chiefly of the
French. I make no manner of queftion,
but the Englifh at this time are infinitely
improved in this way, above the fkill of
former ages; nay, of all countries round
about us, that pretend to greater eloquence.
Yet they have been always judicioufly fpar-
ing, in printing fuch compofures, while
fome other witty nations have tired all their
prefles and readers with them. The truth
is, the letters that pafs between particular
friends, if they are written as they ought
to be, can fcarce ever be fit to fee the light.
They fhould not confift of fulfome com-
pliments,

pliments, or tedious politics, or elaborate
elegancies, or general fancies. But they
should have a native clearnefs and short-
nefs, a domeftical plainnefs, and a peculiar
kind of familiarity ; which can only affect
the humour of thofe to whom they were
intended. The very fame paffages, which
make writings of this nature delightful
amongft friends, will lofe all manner of
tafte when they come to be read by thofe
that are indifferent. In fuch letters the
fouls of men fhould appear undreffed ;
and in that negligent habit, they may be
fit to be feen by one or two in a chamber,
but not to go abroad into the ftreet.

THE laft pieces, that we have from his
hands, are difcourfes, by way of effays, upon
fome of the graveft fubjects that concern
the contentment of a virtuous mind. Thefe
he intended as a real character of his own
thoughts, upon the point of his retirement.
And accordingly you may obferve, that in
the profe of them, there is little curiofity

of

of ornament [c]; but they are written in a
lower and humbler ſtyle than the reſt, and,
as an unfeigned image of his ſoul ſhould be
drawn, without flattery. I do not ſpeak
this to their diſadvantage. For the true
perfection of wit is, to be pliable to all occaſions, to walk or fly, according to the nature of every ſubject. And there is, no
doubt, as much art, to have only plain
conceptions on ſome arguments, as there
is in others to have extraordinary flights.

To theſe, that he has here left ſcarce
finiſhed, it was his deſign to have added
many others. And a little before his death,
he communicated to me his reſolutions, to
have dedicated them all to my Lord St.
Albans, as a teſtimony of his entire reſpects to him; and a kind of apology for
having left human affairs, in the ſtrength
of his age, while he might ſtill have been
ſerviceable to his country. But, though he

[c]—*little curioſity of ornament*] i. e. no quaintneſs
of conceit, and no affectation of language.

was

was prevented in this purpofe by this death, yet it becomes the office of a friend to make good his intentions. I therefore here prefume to make a prefent of them to his Lordfhip. I doubt not but, according to his ufual humanity, he will accept this imperfeft legacy, of the man whom he long honoured with his domeftic converfation. And I am confident his Lordfhip will believe it to be no injury to his fame, that in thefe papers my Lord St. Albans and Mr. Cowley's name fhall be read together by pofterity.

I might, Sir, have made a longer difcourfe of his writings, but that I think it fit to direft my fpeech concerning him by the fame rule by which he was wont to judge of others. In his efteem of other men, he conftantly preferred the good temper of their minds, and honefty of their actions, above all the excellencies of their eloquence or knowledge. The fame courfe I will take in his praife, which chiefly

ought

ought to be fixed on his life.   For that,
he deserves more applause from the most
virtuous men, than for his other abilities
he ever obtained from the learned.

He had indeed a perfect natural good-
ness, which neither the uncertainties of his
condition, nor the largeness of his wit, could
pervert. He had a firmness and strength of
mind, that was of proof against the art of
poetry itself. Nothing vain or fantastical,
nothing flattering or insolent, appeared in
his humour. He had a great integrity and
plainness of manners; which he preserved
to the last, though much of his time was
spent in a nation, and way of life, that is not
very famous for sincerity. But the truth of
his heart was above the corruption of ill
examples: and therefore the sight of them
rather confirmed him in the contrary virtues.

There was nothing affected or singular
in his habit, or person, or gesture. He understood the forms of good-breeding enough

to practife them without burdening himfelf or others.   He never oppreffed any
man's parts, nor ever put any man out of
countenance.   He never had any emulation for fame, or contention for profit
with any man.   When he was in bufinefs,
he fuffered others importunities with much
eafinefs : when he was out of it, he was
never importunate himfelf.   His modefty
and humility were fo great, that, if he had
not had many other equal virtues, they
might have been thought diffimulation.

His converfation was certainly of the
moft excellent kind; for it was fuch as
was rather admired by his familiar friends,
than by ftrangers at firft fight. He furprized
no man at firft with any extraordinary appearance: he never thruft himfelf violently
into the good opinion of his company.
He was content to be known by leifure
and by degrees : and fo the efteem, that
was conceived of him, was better grounded and more lafting.

IN

In his speech, neither the pleasantness excluded gravity, nor was the sobriety of it inconsistent with delight. No man parted willingly from his discourse: for he so ordered it, that every man was satisfied that he had his share. He governed his passions with great moderation. His virtues were never troublesome or uneasy to any. Whatever he disliked in others, he only corrected it by the silent reproof of a better practice.

His wit was so tempered, that no man had ever reason to wish it had been less; he prevented other men's severity upon it by his own: he never willingly recited any of his writings. None but his intimate friends ever discovered he was a great poet, by his discourse. His learning was large and profound, well composed of all ancient and modern knowledge. But it sat exceeding close and handsomely upon him: it was not embossed on his mind, but enamelled.

HE

HE never guided his life by the whifpers or opinions of the world : yet he had a great reverence for a good reputation. He hearkened to fame, when it was a juft cen-furer: but not when an extravagant babler. He was a paffionate lover of liberty and freedom from reftraint both in actions and words: but what honefty others receive from the direction of laws, he had by na-tive inclination ; and he was not behold-ing to other men's wills, but to his own, for his innocence.

HE performed all his natural and civil duties with admirable tendernefs. Hav-ing been born after his father's death, and bred up under the difcipline of his mother, he gratefully acknowledged her care of his education to her death, which was in the eightieth year of her age. For his three brothers he always maintained a conftant affection. And having furvived the two firft, he made the third his heir. In his

long

long dependance on my Lord St. Albans, there never happened any manner of difference between them: except a little at last, because he would leave his service; which only shewed the innocence of the servant, and the kindness of the master. His friendships were inviolable. The same men with whom he was familiar in his youth, were his nearest acquaintance at the day of his death. If the private course of his last years made him contract his conversation to a few, yet he only withdrew, not broke off, from any of the others.

His thoughts were never above nor below his condition. He never wished his estate much larger. Yet he enjoyed what he had with all innocent freedom; he never made his present life uncomfortable, by undue expectations of future things. Whatever disappointments he met with, they only made him understand fortune better, not repine at her the more: his Muse indeed once complained, but never his mind.

He

He was accomplished with all manner of abilities for the greatest businefs ; if he would but have thought fo himfelf.

IF any thing ought to have been changed in his temper and difpofition ; it was his earneft affection for obfcurity and retirement. This, Sir, give me leave to condemn, even to you, who I know agreed with him in the fame humour. I acknowledge he chofe that ftate of life, not out of any poetical rapture, but upon a fteady and fober experience of human things. But, however, I cannot applaud it in him. It is certainly a great difparagement to virtue, and learning itfelf, that thofe very things which only make men ufeful in the world, fhould incline them to leave it. This ought never to be allowed to good men, unlefs the bad had the fame moderation, and were willing to follow them into the wildernefs. But, if the one fhall contend to get out of employment, while the other ftrive to get into it, the affairs of mankind are like to be in

fo

fo ill a pofture, that even the good men themfelves will hardly be able to enjoy their very retreats in fecurity.

YET, I confefs, if any deferved to have this privilege, it ought to have been granted to him, as foon as any man living, upon confideration of the manner in which he fpent the liberty that he got. For he withdrew himfelf out of the crowd, with defires of enlightening and inftructing the minds of thofe that remained in it. It was his refolution in that ftation to fearch into the fecrets of divine and human knowledge, and to communicate what he fhould obferve. He always profeffed, that he went out of the world, as it was man's, into the fame world, as it was nature's, and as it was God's. The whole compafs of the creation, and all the wonderful effects of the divine wifdom, were the conftant profpect of his fenfes and his thoughts. And indeed he entered with great advantage on the ftudies of nature, even as the firft great men of antiquity

tiquity did, who were generally both poets
and philofophers.   He betook himfelf to
its contemplation, as well furnifhed with
found judgement, and diligent obfervation,
and good method to difcover its myfteries, as with abilities to fet it forth in all
its ornaments.

THIS labour about natural fcience was
the perpetual and uninterrupted tafk of
that obfcure part of his life.   Befides this,
we had perfuaded him to look back into
his former ftudies, and to publifh a difcourfe concerning ftyle.   In this he had
defigned to give an account of the proper
forts of writing, that were fit for all manner of arguments, to compare the per-
fections and imperfections of the authors
of antiquity with thofe of this prefent age,
and to deduce all down to the particular
ufe of the Englifh genius and language.
This fubject he was very fit to perform :
it being moft proper for him to be the
judge, who had been the beft practifer.

But he fcarce lived to draw the firft lines
of it. All the footfteps that I can find
remaining of it, are only fome indigefted
characters of ancient and modern authors.
And now for the future, I almoft defpair
ever to fee it well accomplifhed, unlefs you,
Sir, would give me leave to name the man
that fhould undertake it.

But his laft and principal defign, was
that which ought to be the principal to
every wife man ; the eftablifhing his mind
in the faith he profefled. He was in his
practice exactly obedient to the ufe and
precepts of our church. Nor was he inclined to any uncertainty and doubt, as ab-
horring all contention in indifferent things,
and much more in facred. But he beheld
the divifions of Chriftendom : he faw how
many controverfies had been introduced by
zeal or ignorance, and continued by faction.
He had therefore an earneft intention of
taking a review of the original principles
of the primitive Church : believing that
every

every true Chriſtian had no better means to ſettle his ſpirit, than that which was propoſed to ÆNEAS and his followers, to be the end of their wanderings,

" — antiquam exquirite matrem [*d*]."

THIS examination he purpoſed ſhould reach to our Saviour's and the Apoſtles lives, and their immediate ſucceſſors for four or five centuries, till intereſt and policy prevailed over devotion. He hoped to have abſolutely compaſſed it in three or four years; and when that was done, there to have fixed for ever, without any ſhaking or alteration in his judgement. Indeed it was a great damage to our church, that he lived not to perform it. For very much of the primitive light might have been expected from a mind that was endued with the primitive meekneſs and innocence. And beſides, ſuch a work, coming from one that was no divine, might have been very uſeful for this age: where-

[*d*] Virg. Æn. iii. 96.

in

in it is one of the principal cavils againft religion, that it is only a matter of intereft, and only fupported for the gain of a particular profeffion.

BUT alas! while he was framing thefe great things in his thoughts, they were unfortunately cut off, together with his life. His folitude, from the very beginning, had never agreed fo well with the conftitution of his body, as of his mind. The chief caufe of it was, that, out of hafte to be gone away from the tumult and noife of the city, he had not prepared fo healthful a fituation in the country, as he might have done, if he had made a more leifurable choice. Of this he foon began to find the inconvenience at Barn-Elms, where he was afflicted with a dangerous and lingering fever. After that, he fcarce ever recovered his former health, though his mind was reftored to its perfect vigour : as may be feen by his two laft books of plants, that were written fince that time, and may at leaft be compared with the beft of his

other

other works. Shortly after his removal to
Chertfea, he fell into another confuming
difeafe. Having languifhed under this for
fome months, he feemed to be pretty well
cured of its ill fymptoms. But in the
heat of the laft fummer, by ftaying too
long amongft his labourers in the meadows;
he was taken with a violent defluxion, and
ftoppage in his breaft and throat. This
he at firft neglected, as an ordinary cold;
and refufed to fend for his ufual phyfi-
cians, till it was paft all remedies; and fo
in the end, after a fortnight's ficknefs, it
proved mortal to him.

WHo can here, Sir, forbear exclaiming on
the weak hopes and frail condition of human nature? For as long as Mr. COWLEY
was purfuing the courfe of ambition, in an
active life, which he fcarce efteemed his
true life; he never wanted a conftant health,
and ftrength of body. But as foon as ever he
had found an opportunity of beginning indeed to live, and to enjoy himfelf in fecu-

rity, his contentment was firſt broken by
ſickneſs, and at laſt his death was occaſioned
by his very delight in the country and the
fields, which he had long fancied above all
other pleaſures.   But let us not grieve at
this fatal accident upon his account, leſt we
ſhould ſeem to repine at the happy change of
his condition, and not to know that the loſs
of a few years, which he might longer have
lived, will be recompenſed by an immortal memory.   If we complain, let it only
be for our own ſakes : that in him we are
at once deprived of the greateſt natural and
improved abilities, of the uſefulleſt converſation, of the faithfulleſt friendſhip, of a
mind that practiſed the beſt virtues itſelf,
and a wit that was beſt able to recommend
them to others,

His body was attended to Weſtminſter
Abbey by a great number of perſons of
the moſt eminent quality, and followed
with the praiſes of all good and learned
men.   It lies near the aſhes of CHAUCER

and Spenser, the two moſt famous Engliſh poets of former times. But whoever
would do him right, ſhould not only equal
him to the principal ancient wíiters of our
own nation, but ſhould alſo rank his name
amongſt the authors of the true antiquity,
the beſt of the Greeks and Romans.—In
that place there is a monument deſigned
for him, by my Lord Duke of Buckingham, in teſtimony of his affection. And
the King himſelf was pleaſed to beſtow on
him the beſt epitaph, when, upon the news
of his death, his Majeſty declared [e]. *That
Mr. Cowley had not left a better man behind him in England.*

This, Sir, is the account that I thought
fit to preſent the world concerning him.
Perhaps it may be judged, that I have
ſpent too many words on a private man,
and a ſcholar : whoſe life was not remark-

[e]—*his Majeſty declared,* &c.] Which only ſhews,
that the curſe of Persius had fallen upon that
prince—" Virtutem videant, intabeſçantque relictâ."
Sat. iii. 35.

able

able for fuch a variety of events, as are
wont to be the ornaments of this kind of
relations.   I know it is the cuftom of the
world, to prefer the pompous hiftories of
great men, before the greateft virtues of
others, whofe lives have been led in a courfe
lefs illuftrious.   This indeed is the general humour.   But I believe it to be an error in mens judgements.   For certainly
that is a more profitable inftruction, which
may be taken from the eminent goodnefs
of men of lower rank, than that which
we learn from the fplendid reprefentations
of the battles, and victories, and buildings,
and fayings, of great commanders and
princes.   Such fpecious matters, as they
are feldom delivered with fidelity, fo they
ferve but for the imitation of a very few,
and rather make for the oftentation than
the true information of human life. Where-
as it is from the practice of men equal to
ourfelves, that we are more naturally taught
how to command our paffions, to direct
our knowledge, and to govern our actions,

FOR this reaſon, I have ſome hope, that a character of Mr. COWLEY may be of good advantage to our nation. For what he wanted in titles of honour and the gifts of fortune, was plentifully ſupplied by many other excellencies, which make perhaps leſs noiſe, but are more beneficial for example. This, Sir, was the principal end of this long diſcourſe. Beſides this, I had another deſign it it, that only concerns ourſelves ; that, having this picture of his life ſet before us, we may ſtill keep him alive in our memories, and by this means may have ſome ſmall reparation for our inexpreſſible loſs by his death. Sir, I am,

Your moſt humble,

and moſt affectionate ſervant,

T. SPRAT.

ELEGIA

DEDICATORIA,

AD

ILLUSTRISSIMAM ACADEMIAM

CANTABRIGIENSEM.

HOC tibi de nato, dìtiffima mater, egeno
    Exiguum immenfi pignus amoris habe.
Heu, meliora tibi depromere dona volentes
    Aftringit gratas parcior arca manus.
Túne tui poteris vocem hìc agnofcere nati
    Tam malè formatam, diffimilemque tuæ?
Túne hìc materni veftigia facra decoris,
    Tu fpeculum poteris hìc reperire tuum?
Poft longum, dices, Coulëi, fic mihi tempus?
    Sic mihi fperanti, perfide, multa redis?
Quæ, dices, Sagæ Lemuréfque Deæque, nocentes,
    Hunc mihi in infantis fuppofuêre loco?
At tu, fancta parens, crudelis tu quoque, nati
    Ne tractes dextrâ vulnera cruda rudi.

Hei

Hei mihi, quid fato genetrix accedis iniquo?
    Sit fors, fed non fis; ipfa, noverca mihi.
Si mihi natali Mufarum adolefcere in arvo,
    Si benè dilecto luxuriare folo,
Si mihi de doctâ licuiffet pleniùs undâ
    Haurire, ingentem fi fatiare fitim,
Non ego degeneri dubitabilis ore redirem,
    Nec legeres nomen fufa rubore meum.
Scis benè, fcis quæ me tempeftas publica mundi
    Raptatrix veftro fuftulit è gremio,
Nec pede adhuc firmo, nec firmo dente, negati
    Pofcentem querulo murmure lactis opem.
Sic quondam, aërium vento bellante per æquor,
    Cum gravidum autumnum fæva flagellat hyems,
Immatura fuâ velluntur ab arbore poma,
    Et vi victa cadunt; arbor & ipfa gemit.
Nondum fuccus ineft terræ generofus avitæ,
    Nondum fol rofeo redditur ore pater.
O mihi jucundum Grantæ fuper omnia nomen!
    O penitùs toto corde receptus amor!
O pulcræ fine luxu ædes, vitæque beatæ,
    Splendida paupertas, ingenuúfque decor!
O chara ante alias, magnorum nomine regum
    Digna domus! Trini nomine digna Dei!
O nimium Cereris cumulati munere campi,
    Pofthabitis Ennæ quos colit illa jugis!
O facri fontes! & facræ vatibus umbræ,
    Quas recreant avium Pieridúmque chori!
       I   O Camus!

O Camus! Phœbo nullus quo gratior amnis!
  Amnibus auriferis invidiofus inops!
Ah mihi fi veftræ reddat bona gaudia fedis,
  Detque Deus doctâ poffe quiete frui!
Qualis eram, cum me tranquillâ mente fedentem
  Vidifti in ripâ, Came ferene, tuâ;
Mulcentem audifti puerili flumina cantu;
  Ille quidèm immerito, fed tibi gratus erat.
Nam, memini ripâ cum tu dignatus utrâque,
  Dignatum eft totum verba referre nemus.
Tunc liquidis tacitifque fimul mea vita diebus,
  Et fimilis veftræ candida fluxit aquæ.
At nunc cœnofæ luces, atque obice multo
  Rumpitur ætatis turbidus ordo meæ.
Quid mihi Sequanâ opus, Tamefisve aut Thy-
    bridis unda?
  Tu potis es noftram tollere, Came, fitim.
Felix, qui nunquam plus uno viderit amne!
  Quique eadem Salicis littora more colit!
Felix, qui non tentatus fordefcere mundus,
  Et cui pauperies nota nitere poteft!
Tempore cui nullo mifera experientia conftat,
  Ut res humanas fentiat effe nihil!
At nos exemplis fortuna inftruxit opimis,
  Et documentorum fatque fupérque dedit.
Cum capite avulfum diadema, infractáque fceptra,
  Contufáfque hominum forte minante minas,
                                    Parcarum

Parcarum ludos, & non tractabile fatum,
  Et verfas fundo vidimus orbis opes.
Quis poterit fragilem poft talia credere puppim
  Infami fcopulis naufragiifque mari ?
Tu quoque in hoc terræ tremuifti, Academia, motu
  (Nec fruftrà) atque ædes contremuêre tuæ :
Contremuêre ipfæ pacatæ Palladis acres ;
  Et timuít fulmen laurea fanƈta novum.
Ah quanquam iratum, peftem hanc avertere numen,
  Nec faltem bellis ifta licere, velit !
Nos, tua progenies, pereamus ; & ecce, perimus !
  In nos jus habeat : jus habet omne malum.
Tu ftabilis brevium genus immortale nepotum
  Fundes ; nec tibi mors ipfa fuperftes erit :
Semper plena manens uteri de fonte perenni
  Formofas mittes ad mare mortis aquas.
Sic Venus humaná quondam, Dea faucia dextrâ,
  (Namque folent ipfis bella nocere Deis)
Imploravit opem fuperûm, queftúfque cievit,
  Tinxit adorandus candida membra cruor.
Quid quereris ? contemne breves fecura dolores :
  Nam tibi ferre necem vulnera nulla valent.

THE

THE

AUTHOR'S PREFACE

TO

His EDITION in Folio, 1656.

AT my return lately into England [ƒ],
I met by great accident (for such I
account it to be, that any copy of it should
be extant any where so long, unlefs at
his houfe who printed it) a book entituled,
The Iron Age, and published under my
name, during the time of my abfence. I
wondered very much how one who could
be fo foolifh to write fo ill verfes, should
yet be fo wife to fet them forth as another
man's rather than his own ; though perhaps he might have made a better choice,
and not fathered the baftard upon fuch

[ƒ] In 1656.

a perfon,

a perfon, whofe stock of reputation is, I
fear, little enough for maintenance of his
own numerous legitimate off-fpring of that
kind. It would have been much lefs injurious, if it had pleafed the author to put
forth fome of my writings under his own
name, rather than his own under mine :
he had been in that a more pardonable
plagiary, and had done lefs wrong by rob-
bery, than he does by fuch a bounty; for
nobody can be juftified by the imputation even of another's merit ; and our own
coarfe cloaths are like to become us better than thofe of another man, though
never fo rich : but thefe, to fay the truth,
were fo beggarly, that I myfelf was afhamed
to wear them. It was in vain for me, that
I avoided cenfure by the concealment of
my own writings, if my reputation could
be thus executed *in effigie*; and impoffible
it is for any good name to be in fafety,
if the malice of witches have the power
to confume and deftroy it in an image of
their own making. This indeed was fo

ill

ill made, and so unlike, that I hope the
charm took no effect. So that I esteem
myself less prejudiced by it, than by that
which has been done to me since, almost
in the same kind; which is, the publication of some things of mine without my
consent or knowledge, and those so mangled
and imperfect, that I could neither with
honour acknowledge, nor with honesty
quite disavow them.

Of which sort, was a comedy called *The
Guardian*, printed in the year 1650; but
made and acted before the Prince, in his
passage through Cambridge towards York,
at the beginning of the late unhappy war;
or rather neither made nor acted, but
rough-drawn only, and repeated; for the
haste was so great, that it could neither
be revised or perfected by the author, nor
learned without-book by the actors, nor
set forth in any measure tolerably by the
officers of t' e college. After the repre-
sentation (which, I confess, was somewhat

of the lateft) I began to look it over,
and changed it very much, ftriking out
fome whole parts, as that of the poet and
the foldier; but I have loft the copy, and
dare not think it deferves the pains to
write it again, which makes me omit it
in this publication, though there be fome
things in it which I am not afhamed of,
taking the excufe of my age and fmall experience in human converfation when I
made it.   But, as it is, it is only the hafty
firft-fitting of a picture, and therefore like
to refemble me accordingly.

FROM this which has happened to myfelf, I began to reflect on the fortune of
almoft all writers, and efpecially poets,
whofe works (commonly printed after their
deaths) we find ftuffed out, either with
counterfeit pieces, like falfe money put in
to fill up the bag, though it add nothing
to the fum; or with fuch, which, though
of their own coin, they would have called
in themfelves, for the bafenefs of the allay:
whether

whether this proceed from the indifcretion of their friends, who think a vaft heap of ftones or rubbifh a better monument than a little tomb of marble, or by the unworthy avarice of fome ftationers, who are content to diminifh the value of the author, fo they may increafe the price of the book; and, like vintners, with fophifticate mixtures, fpoil the whole veffel of wine, to make it yield more profit. This has been the cafe with SHAKESPEAR, FLETCHER, JONSON, and many others; part of whofe poems I fhould take the boldnefs to prune and lop away, if the care of replanting them in print did belong to me [g]: neither would I make any fcruple to cut off from fome the unneceffary young fuckers, and from others the old withered branches; for a great wit is no more tied to live in a vaft volume, than in a gigantic body; on the contrary, it is commonly more vigorous, the lefs fpace it

[g] The editor's apology for the liberty taken in this edition, is here made by the author himfelf.

animates.

animates.   And, as Statius fays of little
Tydeus [*b*],

—— Totos infufa per artus
Major in exiguo regnabat corpore virtus.

I am not ignorant, that, by faying this of
others, I expofe myfelf to fome raillery,
for not ufing the fame fevere difcretion in
my own cafe, where it concerns me nearer :
But though I publifh here more than in
ftrict wifdom I ought to have done, yet I
have fuppreft and caft away more than I
publifh ; and, for the eafe of myfelf and
others, have loft, I believe too, more than
both.   And upon thefe confiderations I
have been perfuaded to overcome all the
juft repugnances of my own modefty, and
to produce thefe poems to the light and
view of the world ; not as a thing that I
approved of in itfelf, but as a lefs evil,
which I chofe rather than to ftay till it
were done for me by fomebody elfe, either furreptitioufly before, or avowedly af-

[*b*] Stat. Theb. l. i. 416.

ter,

ter, my death: and this will be the more excufable, when the reader fhall know in what refpeéts he may look upon nie as a dead, or at leaft a dying perfon, and upon my Mufe in this aétion, as appearing, like the Emperor CHARLES the Fifth, and affifting at her own funeral.

FOR, to make myfelf abfolutely dead in a poetical capacity, my refolution at prefent is, never to exercife any more that faculty. It is, I confefs, but feldom feen that the poet dies before the man ; for, when we once fall in love with that bewitching art, we do not ufe to court it as a miftrefs, but marry it as a wife, and take it for better or worfe, as an infeparable companion of our whole life. But, as the marriages of infants do but rarely profper, fo no man ought to wonder at the diminution or decay of my affeétion to poefy ; to which I had contraéted myfelf fo much under age, and fo much to my own prejudice in regard of thofe more profitable

F 3 . matches,

matches, which I might have made among the richer fciences. As for the portion which this brings of fame, it is an eftate (if it be any, for men are not oftener deceived in their hopes of widows, than in their opinion of, " Exegi monumentum " ære perennius—") that hardly ever comes in whilft we are living to enjoy it, but is a fantaftical kind of reverfion to our own felves : neither ought any man to envy poets this pofthumous and imaginary happinefs, fince they find commonly fo little in prefent, that it may be truly applied to them, which St. PAUL fpeaks of the firft Chriftians, " If their reward be in " this life, they are of all men the moft " miferable."

AND, if in quiet and flourifhing times they meet with fo fmall encouragement, what are they to expect in rough and troubled ones ? If wit be fuch a plant, that it fcarce receives heat enough to preferve it alive even in the fummer of our cold climate,

climate, how can it choofe but wither in a long and a fharp winter ? A warlike, various, and a tragical age is beft to write of, but worft to write in. And I may, though in a very unequal proportion, affume that to myfelf, which was fpoken by TULLY to a much better perfon, upon occafion of the civil wars and revolutions in his time " Sed in te intuens, Brute, doleo : " cujus in adolefcentiam, per medias laudes, " quafi quadrigis vehentem, tranfverfa in- " currit mifera fortuna reipublicæ [*i*]."

NEITHER is the prefent conftitution of my mind more proper than that of the times for this exercife, or rather divertifement. There is nothing that requires fo much ferenity and chearfulnefs of fpirit ; it muft not be either overwhelmed with the cares of life, or overcaft with the clouds of melancholy and forrow, or fhaken and difturbed with the ftorms of injurious fortune; it muft, like the halcyon, have fair

[*i*] Cic. de Clar. Orator. § 331.

weather

weather to breed in.   The foul muft be
filled with bright and delightful ideas,
when it undertakes to communicate delight
to others; which is the main end of poefy.
One may fee through the ftyle of Ovid de
Trift. the humbled and dejected condition
of fpirit with which he wrote it; there
fcarce remains any footftep of that genius,

—quem nec Jovis ira, nec ignes [*k*], &c.

The cold of the country had ftrucken
through all his faculties, and benumbed
the very feet of his verfes.   He is himfelf,
methinks, like one of the ftories of his
own Metamorphofis ; and, though there
remain fome weak refemblances of OVID
at Rome, it is but, as he fays of NIOBE [*l*],

In vultu color eft fine fanguine: lumina mœftis
Stant immota genis: nihil eft in imagine vivi.——
Flet tamen——

The truth is, for a man to write well, it
is neceffary to be in good humour; nei-

- [*k*] Metam. l. xv. 871.
  [*l*] Metam. l. vi. 304.

ther

ther is wit lefs eclipfed with the unquiet-
nefs of mind, than beauty with the indif-
pofition of body.   So that it is almoft as
hard a thing to be a poet in defpight of
fortune, as it is in defpight of nature. For
my own part, neither my obligations to
the Mufes, nor expeftations from them,
are fo great, as that I fhould fuffer myfelf
on no confiderations to be divorced, or that
I fhould fay like HORACE [*m*],

Quifquis erit vitæ, fcribam, color.

I fhall rathēr ufe his words in another
place [*n*],

Vixi Camenis nuper idoneus,
Et militavi non fine gloriâ :
    Nunc arma, defunctúmque bello
    Barbiton hic paries habebit.

And this refolution of mine does the more
befit me, becaufe my defire has been for
fome years paft (though the execution has
been accidentally diverted) and does ftill

[*m*] Hor. 2 Sat. i. 60.
[*n*] 3 Carm. Ode xxvi.   " Vixi puellis," &c.
                                vehemently

vehemently continue, to retire myfelf to fome of our American plantations, not to feek for gold, or inrich myfelf with the traffic of thofe parts (which is the end of moft men that travel thither; fo that of thefe Indies it is truer than it was of the former,

> Impiger extremos currit mercator ad Indos,
> Per mare pauperiem fugiens—[o])

but to forfake this world for ever, with all the vanities and vexations of it, and to bury myfelf there in fome obfcure retreat (but not without the confolation of letters and philofophy)

> Oblitúfque meorum, oblivifcendus & illis—[p]

as my former author fpeaks too, who has inticed me here, I know not how, into the pedantry of this heap of Latin fentences. And I think Dr. DONNE's *Sun-dyal in a grave* is not more ufelefs and ridiculous, than poetry would be in that retirement.

[o] Hor. 1 Ep. i. 45.
[p] Hor. 1 Ep. xi. 9.

As

As this therefore is in a true fenfe a kind of death to the Mufes, and a real literal quitting of this world; fo, methinks, I may make a juft claim to the undoubted privilege of deceafed poets, which is, to be read with more favour than the living;

Tanti eft ut placeam tibi, perire [q].

HAVING been forced, for my own neceffary juftification, to trouble the reader with this long difcourfe of the reafons why I trouble him alfo with all the reft of the book; I fhall only add fomewhat concerning the feveral parts of it, and fome other pieces, which I have thought fit to rejeët in this publication: as, firft, all thofe which I wrote at fchool, from the age of ten years, till after fifteen; for even fo far backward there remain yet fome traces of me in the little footfteps of a child; which, though they were then looked upon as commendable extravagancies in a boy (men fetting a value upon any kind of

[q] Martial. lib. viii. ep. 69.

fruit

fruit before the ufual feafon of it) yet I would be loth to be bound now to read them all over myfelf; and therefore fhould do ill to expect that patience from others. Befides, they have already paft through feveral editions, which is a longer life than ufes to be enjoyed by infants that are born before the ordinary terms. They had the good fortune then to find the world fo indulgent (for, confidering the time of their production, who could be fo hard-hearted to be fevere? that I fcarce yet apprehend fo much to be cenfured for them, as for not having made advances after-wards proportionable to the fpeed of my fetting out; and am obliged too in a manner by difcretion to conceal and fupprefs them, as promifes and inftruments under my own hand, whereby I ftood engaged for more than I have been able to perform; in which truly if I have failed, I have the real excufe of the honefteft fort of bankrupts, which is, to have been made unfolvable, not fo much by their own neg-
ligence

ligence and ill-hufbandry, as by fome no-
torious accidents and public difafters. In
the next place, 1 have caft away all fuch
pieces as I wrote during the time of the
late troubles, with any relation to the differences that caufed them; as, among
others, three books of the civil war itfelf,
reaching as far as the firft battle of Newbury, where the fucceeding misfortunes of
the party ftopt the work.

As for the enfuing book, it confifts of
four parts. The firft is a Mifcellany of feveral fubjects, and fome of them made
when I was very young, which it is perhaps fuperfluous to tell the reader: I know
not by what chance I have kept copies of
them; for they are but a very few in comparifon of thofe which I have loft; and I
think they have no extraordinary virtue in
them, to deferve more care in prefervation,
than was beftowed upon their brethren;
for which I am fo little concerned, that I
am alhamed of the arrogancy of the word,
when I faid, I had loft them.

THE

THE second, is called, *The Miftrefs*, or *Love-Verfes* ; for fo it is, that poets are fcarce thought freemen of their company, without paying fome duties, and obliging themfelves to be true to love. Sooner or later they muft all pafs through that trial, like fome Mahometan monks, that are bound by their order, once at leaft in their life, to make a pilgrimage to Mecca :

> In furias ignemque ruunt : amor omnibus
> idem [r].

But we muft not always make a judgement of their manners from their writings of this kind; as the Romanifts uncharitably do of BEZA, for a few lafcivious fonnets compofed by him in his youth. It is not in this fenfe that poefy is faid to be a kind of painting ; it is not the picture of the poet, but of things and perfons imagined by him. He may be in his own practice and dif- pofition a philofopher, nay a Stoic, and yet

[r] Virg. Georg. iii. 244.

speak

ſpeak ſometimes with the ſoftneſs of an amorous Sappho,

——ferat & rubus aſper amomum [s].

He profeſſes too much the uſe of fables (though without the malice of deceiving) to have his teſtimony taken even againſt himſelf. Neither would I here be miſunderſtood, as if I affected ſo much gravity, as to be aſhamed to be thought really in love. On the contrary, I cannot have a good opinion of any man, who is not at leaſt capable of being ſo. But I ſpeak it to excuſe ſome expreſſions (if ſuch there be) which may happen to offend the ſeverity of ſupercilious readers: for much exceſs is to be allowed in love, and even more in poetry; ſo we avoid the two unpardonable vices in both, which are obſcenity and profaneneſs, of which I am ſure, if my words be ever guilty, they have ill repreſented my thoughts and intentions. And if, notwithſtanding all

[s] Virg. Ecl. iii. 89.

this,

I

this, the lightnefs of the matter here dif-
pleafe any body; he may find wherewithal
to content his more ferious inclinations in
the weight and height of the enfuing arguments.

FOR, as for the Pindaric Odes (which is
the third part), I am in great doubt whether
they will be underftood by moft readers;
nay, even by very many who are well
enough acquainted with the common roads
and ordinary tracts of poefy. They either
are, or at leaft were meant to be, of that
kind of ftyle which DION. HALICARNAS-
SEUS calls, Μεζαλοφυὲς κ, ἡδὺ μεζα δεινότηζ,
and which he attributes to ALCÆUS: the
digreffions are many, and fudden, and
fometimes long, according to the fafhion of
all lyriques, and of PINDAR above all men
living. The figures are unufual and bold,
even to temerity, and fuch as I durft not
have to do withal in any other kind of
poetry : the numbers are various and ir-
regular, and fometimes (efpecially fome
of

I

of the long ones) feem harfh and uncouth,
if the juft meafures and cadences be not
obferved in the pronunciation. So that
almoft all their fweetnefs and numerofity
(which is to be found, if I miftake not,
in the rougheft, if rightly repeated) lies
in a manner wholly at the mercy of the
reader. I have briefly defcribed the nature of thefe verfes, in the c de entituled,
The Refurrection: and though the liberty
of them may incline a man to beli ve them
eafy to be compofed, yet the undertaker
will find it otherwife—

—Ut fibi quivis
Speret idem; fudet multùm, fruftráquε laboret
Aufus idem [*t*].

I COME now to the laft part, which is
Davideis, or an heroical poem of the troubles of DAVID : which I defigned into
twelve books ; not for the tribes fake, but
after the pattern of our mafter VIRGIL ;
and intended to clofe all with that moft

[*t*] Hor. A. P. 240.

VOL. I.   G   poetical

poetical and excellent elegy of DAVID on
the death of SAUL and JONATHAN : for I
had no mind to carry him quite on to his
anointing at Hebron, becaufe it is the
cuftom of heroic poets (as we fee by the
examples of HOMER and VIRGIL, whom
we fhould do ill to forfake to imitate
others) never to come to the full end of
their ftory; but only fo near, that every
one may fee it; as men commonly play
not out the game, when it is evident that
they can win it, but lay down their cards,
and take up what they have won. This,
I fay, was the whole defign, in which
there are many noble and fertile arguments behind; as the barbarous cruelty
of SAUL to the priefts at Nob, the feveral
flights and efcapes of DAVID, with the
manner of his living in the Wildernefs,
the funeral of SAMUEL, the love of ABIGAL,
the facking of Ziglag, the lofs and reco-
very of DAVID's wives from the Amale-
kites, the witch of Endor, the war with
the Philiftines, and the battle of Gilboa;
all

all which I meant to interweave, upon feveral occafions, with moft of the illuftrious
ftories of the Old Teftament, and to em-
bellifh with the moft remarkable antiqui-
ties of the Jews and of other nations before or at that age.

But I have had neither leifure hitherto,
nor have appetite at prefent, to finifh the
work, or fo much as to revife that part
which is done, with that care which I re-
folved to beftow upon it, and which the
dignity of the matter well deferves. For
what worthier fubject could have been
chofen, among all the treafuries of paft
times, than the life of this young prince;
who, from fo fmall beginnings, through
fuch infinite troubles and oppofitions, by
fuch miraculous virtues and excellencies,
and with fuch incomparable variety of wonderful actions and accidents, became the
greateft monarch that ever fat on the moft
famous throne of the whole earth? Whom
fhould a poet more juftly feek to honour,

than the higheſt perſon who ever honoured his profeſſion? whom a Chriſtian poet, rather than the man after GOD's own heart, and the man who had that ſacred preeminence above all other princes, to be the beſt and mightieſt of that royal race from whence Chriſt himſelf, according to the fleſh, diſdained not to deſcend?

WHEN I conſider this, and how many other bright and magnificent ſubjects of the like nature the holy Scripture affords and proffers, as it were, to poeſy; in the wiſe managing and illuſtrating whereof the glory of God Almighty might be joined with the ſingular utility and nobleſt delight of mankind; it is not without grief and indignation that I behold that divine ſcience employing all her inexhauſtible riches of wit and eloquence, either in the wicked and beggarly flattery of great perſons, or the unmanly idolizing of fooliſh women, or the wretched affectation of ſcurril laughter, or at beſt on the confuſed antiquated

I

antiquated dreams of senselefs fables and metamorphofes. Amongft all holy and confecrated things, which the devil ever ftole and alienated from the fervice of the Deity; as altars, temples, facrifices, prayers, and the like; there is none that he fo univerfally, and fo long ufurpt, as poetry. It is time to recover it out of the tyrant's hands, and to reftore it to the kingdom of God, who is the father of it. It is time to baptize it in Jordan, for it will never become clean by bathing in the water of Damafcus. There wants, methinks, but the converfion of that, and the Jews, for the accomplifhment of the kingdom of Chrift. And as men, before their receiving of the faith, do not without fome carnal reluctancies apprehend the bonds and fetters of it, but find it afterwards to be the trueft and greateft liberty: it will fare no otherwife with this art, after the regeneration of it; it will meet with wonderful variety of new, more beautiful, and more delightful objects; neither

G 3   will

will it want room, by being confined to heaven.

THERE is not so great a lye to be found in any poet, as the vulgar conceit of men, that lying is essential to good poetry. Were there never so wholesome nourishment to be had (but alas, it breeds nothing but diseases) out of these boasted feasts of love and fables; yet, methinks, the un-alterable continuance of the diet should make us nauseate it: for it is almost im-possible to serve up any new dish of that kind. They are all but the cold-meats of the ancients, new-heated, and new set forth. I do not at all wonder that the old poets made some rich crops out of these grounds; the heart of the soil was not then wrought out with continual til-lage: but what can we expect now, who come a gleaning, not after the first reapers, but after the very beggars? Besides, though those mad stories of the gods and heroes seem in themselves so ridi-culous;

culous; yet they were then the whole body (or rather chaos) of the theology of thofe times. They were believed by all, but a few philofophers, and perhaps fome atheifts; and ferved to good purpofe a-mong the vulgar (as pitiful things as they are), in ftrengthening the authority of law with the terrors of confcience, and expecta-tion of certain rewards and unavoidable punifhments. There was no other religion; and therefore that was better than none at all. But to us, who have no need of them, to us, who deride their folly, and are wearied with their impertinencies; they ought to appear no better arguments for verfe, than thofe of their worthy fucceffors, the knights errant. What can we ima-gine more proper for the ornaments of wit or learning in the ftory of DEUCALION than in that of NOAH? Why will not the ac-tions of SAMPSON afford as plentiful mat-ter as the labours of HERCULES? Why is not JEPTHA's daughter as good a wo-man as IPHIGENIA? and the friendfhip of

G 4   DAVID

DAVID and JONATHAN more worthy cele‑
bration than that of THESEUS and PERI‑
THOUS ? Does not the passage of MOSES
and the Israelites into the Holy Land
yield incomparably more poetical variety
than the voyages of ULYSSES or ÆNEAS ?
Are the obsolete thread‑bare tales of Thebes
and Troy half so stored with great, he‑
roical, and supernatural actions (since verse
will needs find or make such), as the wars
of JOSHUA, of the Judges, of DAVID, and
divers others? Can all the transformations
of the gods give such copious hints to
flourish and expatiate on, as the true mi‑
racles of Christ, or of his prophets and
apostles? What do I instance in these few
particulars? All the books of the Bible
are either already most admirable and ex‑
alted pieces of poesy, or are the best mate‑
rials in the world for it,

YET, though they be in themselves so
proper to be made use of for this purpose ;
none but a good artist will know how to
do

do it : neither muſt we think to cut and poliſh diamonds with ſo little pains and ſkill as we do marble. For, if any man deſign to compoſe a ſacred poem, by only turning a ſtory of the Scripture, like Mr. QUARLES'S, or ſome other godly matter, like Mr. HEYWOOD of angels, into rhyme; he is ſo far from elevating of poeſy, that he only abaſes divinity. In brief, he who can write a prophane poem well, may write a divine one better ; but he who can do that but ill, will do this much worſe. The ſame fertility of invention ; the ſame wiſdom of diſpoſition ; the ſame judgement in obſervance of decencies ; the ſame luſtre and vigor of elocution ; the ſame modeſty and majeſty of number ; briefly, the ſame kind of habit, is required to both : only this latter allows better ſtuff; and therefore would look more deform-edly, ill dreſt in it. I am far from aſ-ſuming to myſelf to have fulfilled the duty of this weighty undertaking : but ſure I am, there is nothing yet in our

language

language (nor perhaps in any) that is in any degree anfwerable to the idea that I conceive of it. And I fhall be ambitious of no other fruit from this weak and imperfect attempt of mine, but the opening of a way to the courage and induftry of fome other perfons, who may be better able to perform it thoroughly and fuccefsfully.

THE

THE AUTHOR'S PREFACE

T O

THE CUTTER OF COLEMAN-STREET [*u*].

A COMEDY, called the Guardian, and made by me when I was very young, was acted formerly at Cambridge; and several times after, privately, during the troubles, as I am told, with good approbation, as it has been lately too at

[*u*] This comedy has considerable merit. The dialogue is easy enough, and many of the scenes pleasant. And, though the subject be farcical, and the plot too much in the Spanish taste of intrigue, I should, perhaps, have inserted the *Cutter of Coleman-street* in the present collection, if, agreeably to the plan and purpose of this publication, I could have found room for so long a work. However, the *Preface* could by no means be omitted, as it serves to let us into the writer's character, and is written, throughout, in his own spirit.

Dublin.

Dublin. There being many things in it which I difliked, and finding myfelf for. fome days idle, and alone in the country, I fell upon the changing of it almoft wholly, as now it is, and as it was played fince at his Royal Highnefs's theatre under this new name. It met at the firft repre- fentation with no favourable reception ; and I think there was fomething of faction againft it, by the early appearance of fome mens difapprobation before they had feen enough of it to build their diflike upon their judgement. Afterwards it got fome ground, and found friends, as well as ad- verfaries. In which condition I fhould willingly let it die, if the main imputation under which it fuffered had been fhot only againft my wit or art in thefe matters, and not directed againft the tendereft parts of human reputation, good-nature, good- manners, and piety itfelf.

THE firft clamour, which fome mali- cious perfons raifed, and made a great noife
with,

with, was, that it was a piece intended for abufe and fatire againft the King's party. Good God! againft the King's party? After having ferved it twenty years, during all the time of their misfortunes and afflictions ; I muft be a very rafh and imprudent perfon, if I chofe out that of their reftitution to begin a quarrel with them. I muft be too much a madman to be trufted with fuch an edged tool as comedy. But firft, why fhould either the whole party (as it was once diftinguifhed by that name, which I hope is abolifhed now by univerfal loyalty), or any man of virtue or honour in it, believe themfelves injured, or at all concerned, by the reprefentation of the faults and follies of a few, who in the general divifion of the nation had crouded in among them ? In all mixed numbers (which is the cafe of parties), nay, in the moft entire and continued bodies, there are often fome degenerated and corrupted parts, which may be caft away from that, and even cut off from this unity, with-

out

out any infection of scandal to the remaining body. The church of Rome,
with all her arrogance, and her wide pre-
tences of certainty in all truths, and exemp-
tion from all errors, does not clap on this
enchanted armour of infallibility upon all
her particular subjects, nor is offended at
the reproof of her greatest doctors. We
are not, I hope, become such Puritans our-
selves, as to assume the name of the con-
gregation of the spotless. It is hard for
any party to be so ill as that no good, im-
possible to be so good as that no ill, should
be found among them. And it has been
the perpetual privilege of satire and comedy, to pluck their vices and follies, though
not their persons, out of the sanctuary of
any title. A cowardly ranting soldier, an
ignorant charlatanical doctor, a foolish
cheating lawyer, a silly pedantical scholar,
have always been, and still are, the principal
subjects of all comedies, without any scandal given to those honourable professions,
or even taken by their severest professors.
And,

And, if any good phyfician or divine fhould
be offended with me here, for inveighing
againft a quack, or for finding Deacon
Soaker too often in the butteries, my refpect and reverence to their callings would
make me troubled at their difpleafure, but
I could not abftain from taking them for
very choleric and quarrelfome perfons.
What does this therefore amount to, if it
were true which is objected ? But it is far
from being fo; for the reprefentation of
two fharks about the town (fellows merry
and ingenious enough, and therefore admitted into better companies than they deferve, yet withal two very fcoundrels, which
is no unfrequent character at London),
the reprefentation, I fay, of thefe as pretended officers of the Royal army, was made
for no other purpofe but to fhow the world,
that the vices and extravagances imputed
vulgarly to the cavaliers, were really committed by aliens, who only ufurped that
name, and endeavoured to cover the reproach of their indigency, or infamy of
their

their actions, with so honourable a title.
So that the business was not here to cor-
rect or cut off any natural branches, tho'
never so corrupted or luxuriant, but to separate and cast away that vermin, which,
by sticking so close to them, had done great
and considerable prejudice both to the
beauty and fertility of the tree : and this is
plainly said, and as often inculcated, as if
one should write round about a sign, *This is
a dog, This is a dog*, out of over-much caution lest some might happen to mistake it
for a lion.

THEREFORE, when this calumny could
not hold (for the case is clear, and will
take no colour), some others sought out
a subtler hint, to traduce me upon the same
score; and were angry, that the person whom
I made a true gentleman, and one both of
considerable quality and sufferings in the
royal party, should not have a fair and
noble character throughout, but should
submit, in his great extremities, to wrong
his

his niece for his own relief. This is a re-fined exception, such as I little forsaw, nor should, with the dulness of my usual charity, have found out against another man in twenty years. The truth is, I did not intend the character of a hero, one of exemplary virtue, and, as HOMER often terms such men, unblameable, but an ordinary jovial gentleman, commonly called a good fellow, one not so conscientious as to starve rather than do the least injury, and yet endowed with so much sense of honour, as to refuse, when that necessity was removed, the gain of five thousand pounds, which he might have taken from his niece by the rigour of a forfeiture: and let the franknefs of this latter generosity so expiate for the former frailty, as may make us not ashamed of his company; for, if his true metal is but equal to his allay, it will not indeed render him one of the finest sort of men, but it will make him current, for aught I know, in any party that ever yet was in the world. If you be to chufe

VOL. I.   H   parts

parts for a comedy out of any noble or
elevated rank of perfons, the moft proper
for that work are the worft of that kind.
Comedy is humble of her nature, and
has always been bred low, fo that fhe
knows not how to behave herfelf with the
great and accomplifhed. She does not
pretend to the brifk and bold qualities of
wine, but to the ftomachal acidity of
vinegar; and therefore is beft placed among
that fort of people which the Romans
call, *The lees of* ROMULUS. If I had defigned here the celebration of the virtues
of our friends, I would have made the
fcene nobler where I intended to erect
their ftatues. They fhould have ftood in
odes, and tragedies, and epic poems (neither have I totally omitted thofe great
teftimonies of my efteem of them)—" Sed
" nunc non erat his locus," &c.

And fo much for this little fpiny objection, which a man cannot fee without a
magnifying-glafs. The next is enough to
knock

knock a man down, and accufes me of no lefs than prophanenefs. Prophane, to deride the hypocrify of thofe men whofe fkulls are not yet bare upon the gates fince the public and juft punifhment of it ? But there is fome imitation of Scripture-phrafes: God forbid ; there is no reprefentation of the true face of Scripture, but only of that vizard which thefe hypocrites (that is, by interpretation, actors with a vizard) draw upon it. Is it prophane to fpeak of HARRISON's return to life again, when fome of his friends really profeffed their belief of it; and he himfelf had been faid to promife it ? A man may be fo imprudently fcrupulous as to find prophanenefs in any thing, either faid or written, by applying it under fome fimilitude or other to fome expreffions in Scripture. This nicety is both vain and endlefs. But I call God to witnefs, that, rather than one tittle fhould remain among all my writings, which, according to my fevereft judgement, fhould be found guilty of the crime objected, I

would

would myfelf burn and extinguifh them all together. Nothing is fo deteftably lewd and wretchlefs as the derifion of things facred; and would be in me more unpardonable than any man elfe, who have endeavoured to root out the ordinary weeds of poetry, and to plant it almoft wholly with divinity. I am fo far from allowing any loofe or irreverent expreffions, in matters of that religion which I believe, that I am very tender in this point, even for the groffeft errors of confcientious perfons; they are the propereft object (methinks) both of our pity and charity too; they are the innocent and white fectaries, in comparifon of another kind, who engraft pride upon ignorance, tyranny upon liberty, and upon all their herefies, treafon and rebellion. Thefe are principles fo deftructive to the peace and fociety of mankind, that they deferve to be purfued by our ferious hatred; and the putting a mafk of fanctity upon fuch devils, is fo ridiculous, that it ought to be expofed to contempt

contempt and laughter. They are indeed prophane, who counterfeit the foftnefs of the voice of holinefs, to difguife the rough-nefs of the hands of impiety; and not they, who, with reverence to the thing which others diffemble, deride nothing but their diffimulation. If fome piece of an admirable artift fhould be ill copied, even to ridiculoufnefs, by an ignorant hand; and another painter fhould undertake to draw that copy, and make it yet more ridicu-lous, to fhew apparently the difference of the two works, and deformity of the latter; will not every man fee plainly, that the abufe is intended to the foolifh imitation, and not to the excellent original? I might fay much more, to confute and confound this very falfe and malicious accufation; but this is enough, I hope, to clear the mat-ter, and is, I am afraid, too much for a pre-face to a work of fo little confideration.

As for all other objections, which have been, or may be made againft the invention

H 3　　　　　　　or

or elocution, or any thing elfe which comes under the critical jurifdiction ; let it ftand or fall as it can anfwer for itfelf, for I do not lay the great ftrefs of my reputation upon a ftructure of this nature, much lefs upon the flight reparations only of an old and unfafhionable building.　There is no writer but may fail fometimes in point of wit ; and it is no lefs frequent for the auditors to fail in point of judgement.　I perceive plainly, by daily experience, that Fortune is miftrefs of the theatre, as TULLY fays it is of all popular affemblies. No man can tell fometimes from whence the invifible winds rife that move them.　There are a multitude of people, who are truly and only fpectators at a play, without any ufe of their underftanding; and thefe carry it fometimes by the ftrength of their numbers.　There are others, who ufe their underftandings too much; who think it a fign of weaknefs and ftupidity, to let any thing pafs by them unattacked, and that the honour of their judgements (as fome

　　　　　　　　　　　　　　brutals

brutals imagine of their courage) confifts in quarrelling with every thing. We are therefore wonderful wife men, and have a fine bufinefs of it, we, who fpend our time in poetry: I do fometimes laugh, and am often angry with myfelf, when I think on it; and if I had a fon inclined by nature to the fame folly, I believe I fhould bind him from it, by the ftricteft conjurations of a paternal blefling. For what can be more ridiculous, than to labour to give men delight, whilft they labour, on their part, more earneftly, to take offence? To expofe one's felf voluntarily and frankly to all the dangers of that narrow paflage to unprofitable fame, which is defended by rude multitudes of the ignorant, and by armed troops of the malicious? If we do ill, many difcover it, and all defpife us; if we do well, but few men find it out, and fewer entertain it kindly. If we commit errors, there is no pardon; if we could do wonders, there would be but little thanks, and that too extorted from unwilling givers.

H 4

BUT

BUT some perhaps may say, Was it not always thus ? do you expect a particular privilege, that was never yet enjoyed by any poet ? were the ancient Grecian, or noble Roman authors, was VIRGIL himself, exempt from this possibility,

Qui melior multis, quàm tu, fuit, improbe, rebus [*];

who was, in many things, thy better far, thou impudent pretender; as was said by LUCRETIUS to a person, who took it ill that he was to die, though he had seen so many do it before him, who better deserved immortality: and this is to repine at the natural condition of a living poet, as he did at that of a living mortal. I do not only acknowledge the pre-eminence of VIRGIL (whose footsteps I adore), but submit to many of his Roman brethren; and I confess, that even they in their own times, were not so secure from the assaults of de-

[*] Lucr. iii. 1039.

traction

traction (though HORACE brags at laft,

Jam dente minus mordeor invido [*y*];

but then the barkings of a few were drowned in the applaufe of all the reft of the
world, and the poifon of their bitings ex-
tinguifhed by the antidote of great rewards
and great encouragements, which is a way
of curing now out of ufe ; and I really
profefs, that I neither expect, nor think I
deferve it. Indolency would ferve my turn
inftead of pleafure : but the cafe is not fo
well ; for, though I comfort myfelf with
fome affurance of the favour and affection
of very many candid and good-natured
(and yet too judicious and even critical)
perfons ; yet this I do affirm, that from
all which I have written I never received
the leaft benefit, or the leaft advantage,
but, on the contrary, have felt fometimes
the effects of malice and misfortune.

[*y*] 4 Carm. iii. 16.

POEMS

P O E M S

O F

MR. A. COWLEY.

I.

THE MOTTO.

Tentanda via eſt, &c. VIRG.

WHAT ſhall I do to be for ever known,
 And make the age to come my own?
 [a] * * * *
Hence all the flattering vanities, that lay
 Nets of roſes in the way.
Hence the deſire of honours, or eſtate;
 And all that is not above fate.
Hence love himſelf, that tyrant of my days,
 Which intercepts my coming praiſe.

[a] Some lines of the original are left out.

Come,

Come, my beſt friends, my books, and lead me on;
    'Tis time that I were gone.
Welcome, great Stagirite, and teach me now
    All I was born to know.
Thy ſcholar's vict'ries thou doſt far out-do:
    He conquer'd th'earth; the whole world, you[b].
Welcome, learn'd Cicero, whoſe bleſt tongue and wit
    Preſerves Rome's greatneſs yet.
Thou art the firſt of orators; only he,
    Who beſt can praiſe thee, next muſt be [c].
Welcome the Mantuan ſwan, Virgil the wiſe,
    Whoſe verſe walks higheſt, but not flies [d].

[b] *He conquer'd th' earth; the whole world, you*] *Earth,*
means this habitable globe.; *world,* the ſyſtem of uni-
verſal nature. But the compliment is not a little extravagant! like that of Mr. Pope to Newton—
    " God ſaid, Let Newton be, and *all* was light"
—for which the Poet is very juſtly reprehended by his
learned Commentator.

[c]   ——*only he,*
Who beſt can praiſe thee, next muſt be.] i. e. he muſt be *only*
next; for none but Cicero himſelf was equal to the ſubject. The poet glances at what Livy ſaid of the great
Roman orator—" vir magnus, acer, memorabilis, et *in*
" *cujus laudes ſequendas Cicerone laudatore opus fuerit.*" A
fragment, preſerved by the elder Seneca.

[d] *Whoſe verſe walks higheſt, but not flies.*] i. e. which
keeps within the limits of nature, and is ſublime without
                                    Who

Who brought green poefy to her perfect age;
　　And made that art, which was a rage.
Tell me, ye mighty three, what fhall I do ,
　　To be like one of you.
But ye have climb'd the mountain's top, there fit
　　On the calm flourifhing head of it,
And, whilft with wearied fteps we upward go,
　　See us, and clouds below.

II.

O　　D　·　E.

ON WIT.

I.

TELL me, O tell, what kind of thing is wit,
　　Thou, who mafter art of it.

being extravagant. Virgil's *epic* Mufe is here juftly
characterized: the *Lyric*, is a fwan of another fpecies,
of which the poet fays nobly, elfewhere—
　　" Lo, how th' obfequious wind and fwelling air
　　　" The Theban fwan does upwards bear
　　" Into the walks of clouds, where he does play,
　" And with extended wings opens his liquid way."
　　　　　　Pindaric Odes. *The praife of Pindar.*

For the firſt matter loves variety leſs;
Leſs women love't, either in love or dreſs [*e*].
    A thouſand different ſhapes it bears,
    Comely in thouſand ſhapes appears.
Yonder we ſaw it plain ; and here 'tis now,
Like ſpirits in a place, we know not how.

2.

London, that vents of falſe ware ſo much ſtore,
    In no ware deceives us more.
For men, led by the colour and the ſhape,
Like Zeuxes' birds, fly to the painted grape;
    Some things do through our judgement paſs,
    As through a multiplying glaſs.
And ſometimes if the objeſt be too far,
We take a falling meteor for a ſtar.

3.

Hence 'tis, a wit, that greateſt word of fame,
    Grows ſuch a common name.

[*e*] We ſhould now ſay, to avoid the diſagreeable
contraſtion,—
    " Leſs women love *it, or* in love, or dreſs."
—But our poet *affeſted* theſe contraſtions, and, if we may
believe the writer of his life, fancied they gave a ſtrength
and energy to his verſe. The truer reaſon for his uſe of
them was, that he found them in faſhion.

                     And

And wits by our creation they become,
Juft fo, as titular bifhops made at Rome.
    'Tis not a tale, 'tis not a jeft
    Admir'd with laughter at a feaft,
Nor florid talk, which can that title gain ;
The proofs of wit for ever muft remain.

4.

'Tis not to force fome lifelefs verfes meet
    With their five gouty feet.
All every where, like man's, muft be the foul,
And reafon the inferior powers controul.
    Such were the numbers, which could call
    The ftones into the Theban wall.
Such miracles are ceas'd ; and now we fee
No towns or houfes [f] rais'd by poetry.

5.

Yet, 'tis not to adorn, and gild each part;
    That fhows more coft, than art.
Jewels at nofe and lips but ill appear ;
Rather, than all things, wit, let none be there.
    Several lights will not be feen,
    If there be nothing elfe between.

[f] *Houfes*] Here ufed in the double fenfe of *houfes*,
properly fo called, and of *families.*

I

Men

Men doubt, becaufe they ftand fo thick i'th' fky,
If thofe be ftars, which paint the galaxy [g].

6.

'Tis not, when two like words make up one noife;
    Jefts for Dutch men, and Englifh boys.
In which who finds out wit, the fame may fee
In anagrams and acroftics, poetry.
    Much lefs can that have any place
    At which a virgin hides her face;
Such drofs the fire muft purge away; 'tis juft,
The author blufh there, where the reader muft.

7.

'Tis not fuch lines as almoft crack the ftage,
    When Bajazet begins to rage.

[g] This idea has been borrowed by Mr. Addifon,
and applied, with much elegance, to our poet himfelf.
For, fpeaking of Mr. Cowley's wit, he fays—
   " One glitt'ring thought no fooner ftrikes our eyes
   " With filent wonder, but new wonders rife:
   " As in the milky way a fhining white
   " O'erflows the heav'ns with one continued light;
   " That not a fingle ftar can fhew his rays,
   " Whilft jointly all promote the common blaze."
          Account of Englifh poets, to Mr. H. S.
                    Nor

Nor a tall metaphor in the bombaſt way,
Nor the dry chips of ſhort-lung'd Seneca [h].
    Nor upon all things to obtrude
    And force ſome odd ſimilitude.
What is it then, which, like the power divine,
We only can by negatives define? [i]

III.

On the Death of Mr. JORDAN,

Second Maſter at Weſtminſter-School.

HERE lies the maſter of my tender years,
   The guardian of my parent's [k] hope and fears,

[h] —ſhort-lung'd Seneca.] Meaning his ſhort ſentences, as if he had not breath enough to ſerve him for longer—anhelanti ſimilis—Yet, in another ſenſe, he is, perhaps, the moſt long-winded author of antiquity. For, as Mr. Bayle has well obſerved, "Il n'y a guere d'ecrivain dont le verbiage ſoit plus grand que celui de Seneque: Cicero mettroit dans une periode de ſix lignes ce que Seneque dit dans ſix periodes qui tiennent huit ou neuf lignes." Lettres, t. ii.. p. 1502.

[i] The two concluding ſtanzas of this ode are omitted.

[k]—my parent's] That is of his mother's, under whoſe diſcipline he was bred; for he was born (Dr. Sprat tells us) after his father's death.

Whofe government ne'er ftood me in a tear;
All weeping was referv'd to fpend it here.
He pluck'd from youth the follies and the crimes
And built up men againft the future times;
For deeds of age are in their caufes then,
And though he taught but boys, he made the men.
Hence 'twas, a mafter, in thofe ancient days
When men fought knowledge firft, and by it praife,
Was a thing full of reverence, profit, fame;
Father itfelf was but a fecond name.
And if a Mufe hereafter fmile on me,
And fay, " Be thou a poet," men fhall fee
That none could a more grateful fcholar have;
For what I ow'd his life, I'll pay his grave [*l*].

IV.

On the Death of Mr. WILLIAM HERVEY [*m*].

" Immodicis brevis eft ætas, & rara feneftus."
MART. L. VI. Ep. xxix.

I.

]T was a difmal, and a fearful night,
Scarce could the morn drive on th'unwilling light,

[*l*] The reft of this poem (one of thofe which were
written, as he fays, *when he was very young)* is fuppreffed.
[*m*] *Mr. William Hervey.*] The author's beloved
I   When

When fleep, death's image, left my troubled breaft,
  By fomething, liker death, poffeft.
My eyes with tears did uncommanded flow,
  And on my foul hung the dull weight
  Of fome intolerable fate.
What bell was that ? Ah me! too much I know.

2.

My fweet companion, and my gentle peer,
Why haft thou left me thus unkindly here,
Thy end for ever, and my life to moan ;
  O thou haft left me all alone!
Thy foul and body, when death's agony
  Befieg'd, around, thy noble heart,
  Did not with more reluctance part,
Than I, my deareft friend, do part from thee.

3.

My deareft friend, would I had dy'd for thee [n] !
Life and this world henceforth will tedious be.

friend.—This poem came from the heart, and is therefore more natural and pleafing than moft others in the
collection. Unluckily, it occafioned the poet's introduction to Lord St. Albans [fee Life, p. 8]; that is,
it ruined his fortune.

  [n]—*would I had dy'd for thee !*] From 2 Sam. xviii.
33.

Nor ſhall I know hereafter what to do,
    If once my griefs prove tedious too.
Silent and ſad I walk about all day,
      As ſullen ghoſts ſtalk ſpeechleſs by,
      Where their hid treaſures lye:
Alas, my treaſure's gone; why do I ſtay?

4.

He was my friend, the trueſt friend on earth;
A ſtrong and mighty influence join'd our birth [o].
Nor did we envy the moſt ſounding name
    By friendſhip giv'n of old to fame.
None but his brethren he, and ſiſters knew,
      Whom the kind youth preferr'd to me:
      And ev'n in that we did agree;
For much above myſelf I lov'd them, too.

5.

Say, for you ſaw us, ye immortal lights,
How oft unwearied have we ſpent the nights;
Till the Ledæan ſtars, ſo fam'd for love,
    Wonder'd at us from above!

[o] —*join'd our birth.*] In this and the following
ſtanza the poet has copied Perſius, Sat. v.; but with
freedom and ſpirit.

We

We fpent them not in toys, in lufts, or wine;
 But fearch of deep philofophy,
  Wit, eloquence, and poetry,
Arts which I lov'd, for they, my friend, were thine.

6.

Ye fields of Cambridge, our dear Cambridge, fay,
Have you not feen us walking every day?
Was there a tree about, which did not know
 The love betwixt us two?
Henceforth, ye gentle trees, for ever fade;
 Or your fad branches thicker join,
  And into darkfome fhades combine,
Dark, as the grave, wherein my friend is laid.

7.

Henceforth, no learned youths beneath you fing,
Till all the tuneful birds to' your boughs they bring:
No tuneful birds play with their wonted chear,
 And call the learned youths to hear;
No whiftling winds through the glad branches fly;
 But all with fad folemnity,
  Mute and unmoved be,
Mute as the grave, wherein my friend does lye.

I 3

8. To

8.

To him my Mufe made hafte with every ftrain,
Whilft it was new, and warm yet from the brain.
He lov'd my worthlefs rhimes, and like a friend[p],
   Would find out fomething to commend.
Hence now, my Mufe, thou canft not me delight;
   Be this my lateft verfe
   With which I now adorn his hearfe ;
And this my grief, without thy help, fhall write.

9.

Had I a wreath of bays about my brow,
I fhould contemn that flourifhing honour now,
Condemn it to the fire, and joy to hear
   It rage and crackle there.
Inftead of bays, crown with fad cyprefs me ;
   Cyprefs, which tombs does beautify :
   Not Phœbus griev'd fo much as I,
For him, who firft was made that mournful tree.

[p]— *like a friend*]
      —— " each finding, like a friend,
" Something to blame, and fomething to commend."
                 Pope, to Mr. Jervas.
                  10. Large

10.

Large was his foul [q]; as large a foul, as e'er
Submitted to inform a body here.
High as the place 'twas fhortly in heav'n to have,
But low, and humble as his grave:
So high; that all the virtues there did come
As to their chiefeft feat
Confpicuous, and great;
So low, that for me too it made a room.

11.

He fcorn'd this bufy world below, and all
That we, miftaken mortals, pleafure call;
Was fill'd with innocent gallantry and truth,
Triumphant o'er the fins of youth.
He, like the ftars, to which he now is gone,
That fhine with beams like flame,
Yet burn not with the fame,
Had all the light of youth, of the fire none.

12.

Knowledge he only fought, and fo foon caught,
As if for him knowledge had rather fought.

[q] Mr. Gray feems to have had his eye on this line
when he wrote that verfe, in his *Epitaph*—
  " *Large* was his bounty, and his *foul* fincere."

Nor did more learning ever crowded lie
    In such a short mortality.
Whene'er the skilful youth discours'd or writ,
    Still did the notions throng
    About his eloquent tongue,
Nor could his ink flow faster than his wit.

13.

So strong a wit did nature to him frame,
As all things, but his judgement, overcame;
His judgement like the heav'nly moon did show,
    Temp'ring that mighty sea below.
Oh, had he liv'd in learning's world, what bound
    Would have been able to controul
    His over-powering soul ?
We've loft in him arts, that not yet are found[r].

14.

His mirth was the pure spirits of various wit,
Yet never did his God or friends forget.
And, when deep talk and wisdom came in view,
    Retir'd, and gave to them their due :

[r] — *arts that not yet are found.*]
    " And worlds applaud, that must not yet be found."
                Pope, Eff. on Crit. ver. 194.
                            For

For the rich help of books he always took,
 Though his own fearching mind before
 Was fo with notions written o'er,
As if wife nature had made that her book.

15.

So many virtues join'd in him, as we
Can fcarce pick here and there in hiftory.
More than old writers' practice e'er could reach
 As much as they could ever teach :
Thefe did religion, queen of virtue, fway
 And all their facred motions fteer,
 Juft like the firft and higheft fphere,
Which wheels about, and turns all heav'n one way.

16.

With as much zeal, devotion, piety,
He always liv'd, as other faints do die.
Still with his foul fevere account he kept,
 Weeping all debts out, ere he flept.
Then down in peace and innocence he lay,
 Like the fun's laborious light,
 Which ftill in water fets at night,
Unfullied with his journey of the day.

17. Won-

17.

Wondrous young man, why wert thou made so good,
To be snatcht hence, ere better underftood?
Snatcht, before half of thee enough was feen!
    Thou, ripe; and yet thy life, but green!
Nor could thy friends take their laft fad farewel;
      But danger and infectious death
      Malicioufly feiz'd on that breath,
Where life, fpirit, pleafure, always us'd to dwell.

18.

But happy thou, ta'en from this frantic age,
Where ignorance and hypocrify does rage!
A fitter time for heav'n no foul e'er chofe,
    The place now only free from thofe.
There 'mong the bleft thou doft for ever fhine,
      And wherefoe'er thou cafts thy view
      Upon that white and radiant crew,
See'ft not a foul cloath'd with more light than thine.

19.

And, if the glorious faints ceafe not to know
Their wretched friends, who fight with life below;
Thy flame to me does ftill the fame abide,
    Only more pure and rarified.

                There,

There, whilſt immortal hymns thou doſt rehearſe,
   Thou doſt with holy pity ſee
   Our dull and earthly poeſy,
Where grief and miſery can be join'd with verſe[*s*].

V.

TO THE LORD FALKLAND,

For his ſafe Return from the *Northern Expe-*
dition againſt the SCOTS [*t*].

GREAT is thy charge, O North; be wiſe and juſt;
  England commits her Falkland to thy truſt;

[*s*] *Where grief and miſery can be join'd with verſe.*]
Rightly made the diſtinction of *earthly poeſy* ; for the *hea-*
venly (if we ſuppoſe poetry to have any place there) can
only be employed on themes of *joy and happineſs.*—But
the poet had a further meaning in this fine line, to in-
ſinuate the prepoſterous levity and vanity of *earthly poets,*
who can afford to be *witty* even on their own *miſeries.*
This cenſure, falling firſt upon himſelf, has the more
grace.

[*t*] *againſt the Scots.*] In 1639. Conſequently the poet
was then in his 21ſt year. But the chief reaſon for
giving theſe verſes to the Lord Falkland a place in the
preſent collection, is, for the ſake of perpetuating the me-

Return

Return him fafe.   Learning would rather choofe
Her Bodley, or her Vatican, to lofe.
All things, that are but writ or printed there,
In his unbounded breaft engraven are.
There all the fciences together meet,
And every art does all her kindred greet,
Yet juftle not, nor quarrel ; but as well
Agree, as in fome common principle,
So, in an army govern'd right, we fee
(Though out of feveral countries rais'd it be)
That all their order and their place maintain,
The Englifh,Dutch,the Frenchmen,and theDane.
So thoufand diverfe fpecies fill the air,
Yet neither croud nor mix confus'dly there;
Beafts, houfes, trees, and men together lye,
Yet enter undifturb'd into the eye.

mory of the author's *entire friendfhip* with that virtuous
and accomplifhed nobleman—*a friendfhip contraĉted*, as
Dr. Sprat tells us, *by the agreement of their learning and
manners.*—It is remarkable, that we find no compliment
addrefled by Mr. Cowley to the duke of Buckingham, or
the earl of St. Albans.   He fuppofed, without doubt,
that he had done honour enough to thofe lords (fome will
think, too much) in permitting them to be his patrons:
    " Enough for half the greateft of thofe days
    " To 'fcape his cenfure, not expeĉt his praife."
                                        . Pope,
                                          And

And this great prince of knowledge is by fate
Thruſt into th' noiſe and buſineſs of a ſtate.
All virtues, and ſome cuſtoms [*u*], of the court,
Other mens labour, are at leaſt his ſport.
Whilſt we, who can no action undertake,
Whom idleneſs itſelf might learned make,
Who hear of nothing, and as yet ſcarce know
Whether the Scots in England be or no,
Pace dully on, oft tire, and often ſtay,
Yet ſee his nimble Pegaſus fly away.
'Tis nature's fault, who did thus partial grow,
And her eſtate of wit on one beſtow :
Whilſt we, like younger brothers, get at beſt
But a ſmall ſtock, and muſt work out the reſt.
How could he anſwer't, ſhould the ſtate think fit
To queſtion a monopoly of wit [*w*] ?

[*u*] —*ſome* cuſtoms] The expreſſion is remarkable,
and implies that not *all* the cuſtoms of Charles the Firſt's
court were ſuch as would be approved by a man of virtue.
If any are curious to know what thoſe cuſtoms were, they
may have their curioſity in part gratified, by turning
to two remarkable letters of Lady Leiceſter and Lord
Robert Spencer, in the collection of the Sidney papers,
vol. ii. p. 472, and p. 668.

[*w*] — *queſtion a monopoly of wit ?*] As it had done
many *other* monopolies. The alluſion is not ſo far
fetched as it ſeems.

Such

T

Such is the man, whom we require the fame
We lent the North; untoucht, as is his fame.
He is too good for war, and ought to be
As far from danger, as from fear he's free [x].
Those men alone (and those are useful, too)
Whose valour is the only art they know,
Were for sad war and bloody battles born;
Let them the state defend, and he adorn.

VI.

On the Death of Sir Anthony Vandike, the famous Painter.

VANDIKE is dead; but what bold Muse shall
                dare
(Tho' poets in that word [y] with painters share)

[x] — *as from fear he's free.*]   Yet it was, in part, to
vindicate himself from the *imputation* of this fear, that he
always put himself in the way of *danger*, and in the end,
threw away his valuable life at the battle of Newbury.

[y] — *in that word*] Namely, *dare*; alluding to Horace,
        " — pictoribus atque poetis
   " *Quidlibet audendi* semper fuit æqua potestas."
                                A. P. ver. 11.

                                T' ex-

T'exprefs her fadnefs? Poefy muft become
An art like painting here, an art, that's dumb.
Let's all our folemn grief in filence keep,
Like fome fad picture, which he made to weep,
Or thofe who faw't; for none his works could view
Unmov'd with the fame paffions which he drew.
His pieces fo with their live objects ftrive,
That both, or pictures feem, or both alive.
Nature herfelf, amaz'd, does doubting ftand,
Which is her own, and which the painter's hand;
And does attempt the like with lefs fuccefs,
When her own work in twins fhe would exprefs.
His all-refembling pencil did out-pafs
The mimic imagery of looking-glafs.
Nor was his life lefs perfect, than his art:
Nor was his hand lefs erring than his heart [z].
There was no falfe or fading colour there;
The figures fweet and well-proportion'd were.
Moft other men, fet next to him in view,
Appear'd more fhadows than the men he drew.
Thus ftill he liv'd, till heaven did for him call,
Where reverend Luke falutes him firft of all:

[z]—*than his heart.*] A noble eulogy of this extraordinary man! and, if report fays true, a very juft
one.

Where

Where he beholds new fights, divinely fair;
And could almoft wifh for his pencil there;
Did he not gladly fee how all things fhine.
Wondroufly painted in the mind divine [*a*],
Whilft he, for ever ravifh'd with the fhow,
Scorns his own art, which we admire below.

    Only his beauteous lady [*b*] ftill he loves;
(The love of heavenly objects heaven improves)
He fees bright angels in pure beams appear
And thinks on her he left fo like them here,
And you, fair widow, who ftay here alive,
Since he fo much rejoices, ceafe to grieve.
Your joys and griefs were wont the fame to be;
Begin not now, bleft pair, to difagree.
No wonder, death mov'd not his generous mind:
You, and a new-born you, he left behind.
Even fate exprefs'd his love to his dear wife,
And let him end your picture with his life.

    [*a*] —*in the mind divine,*] A platonic idea, which
Malbranche and our Norris have rendered fo famous.
    [*b*] — *his beauteous lady*] A lady, of diftinguifhed
quality, as well as beauty, daughter to the Lord Ru-
theu, Earl of Gowry.

VII. To

VII.

To Sir WILLIAM DAVENANT:

Upon his Two Firſt Books of GONDIBERT,
finiſhed before his Voyage to America.

METHINKS, heroic poeſy, till now,
Like ſome fantaſtic fairy-land, did ſhow;
Gods, devils, nymphs, witches, and gyants race,
And all, but man, in man's chief work had place.
Thou, like ſome worthy knight, with ſacred arms
Doſt drive the monſters thence, and end the charms;
Inſtead of theſe, doſt men and manners plant,
The things, which that rich ſoil did chiefly want.
Yet even thy mortals do their gods excell,
Taught by thy Muſe to fight and love ſo well.
    By fatal hands whilſt preſent empires fall,
Thine from the grave paſt monarchies recall.
So much more thanks from human kind does merit
The poet's fury, than the zealot's ſpirit.
And from the grave thou mak'ſt this empire riſe,
Not, like ſome dreadful ghoſt, t'affright our eyes,
But with more luſtre and triumphant ſtate,
Than when it crown'd at proud Verona ſate.

So will our God rebuild man's perifh'd frame,
And raife him up much better, yet the fame [c] :
So god-like poets do paft things rehearfe ;
Not change, but heighten, nature by their verfe.
    With fhame, methinks, great Italy muft fee
Her conquerors rais'd to life again by thee.
Rais'd by fuch powerful verfe, that ancient Rome
May blufh no lefs to fee her wit o'ercome.
Some men their fancies, like their faith, derive [d];
And think all ill but that, which Rome does give.
The marks of old and catholic would find,
To the fame chair would truth and fiction bind.
Thou in thofe beaten paths difdain'ft to tread,
And fcorn'ft to live by robbing of the dead.

[c] *So will—yet the fame.*] It is pleafant to fee how
the wits catch their ideas from each other. Mr. Pope,
in a letter of compliment to a friend, who had done
much honour to his *Effay on Man*, expreffes himfelf in
thefe words—" It is indeed the fame fyftem as mine,
" but illuftrated with a ray of your own ; *as they fay*
" *our natural body is the fame ftill, when it is glorified.*"
Works, vol. ix. Letter xcvii.
    [d] *Some men their fancies, like their faith, derive,*]

    " Thus wit, like faith, by each man is apply'd
    " To one fmall fect ; and all are damn'd befide."
                        Effay on Crit. ver. 396.

Since time does all things change, thou think'ft not fit
This latter age fhould fee all new, but wit.
Thy fancy, like a flame, its way does make,
And leave bright tracks for following pens to take.
Sure 'twas this noble boldnefs of the Mufe
Did thy defire to feek new worlds [*e*] infufe;
And ne'er did heav'n fo much a voyage blefs,
If thou canft plant but there, with like fuccefs.

VIII.

On the Death of Mr. CRASHAW.

POET and Saint! to thee alone are given
  The two moft facred names of earth and heaven;
The hard and rareft union, which can be,
Next that of Godhead with humanity.
Long did the Mufes banifh'd flaves abide,
And built vain pyramids to mortal pride;

[*e*] —*new worlds*] This alludes to Sir William's project of a fettlement at Virginia; which, however, had
no better fuccefs than the poetical project, which his
friend here celebrates.

Like

Like Mofes thou (though fpells and charms with-
  ftand)
Haft brought them nobly home back to their Holy
  Land.

 Ah wretched we, poets of earth ! but thou
Wert, living, the fame poet, which thou'rt now.
Whilft angels fing to thee their airs divine,
And joy in an applaufe fo great as thine ;
Equal fociety with them to hold,
Thou need'ft not make new fongs, but fay the old.
And they (kind fpirits !) fhall all rejoice to fee
How little lefs than they, exalted man may be.
Still the old heathen gods in numbers dwell,
The heavenlieft thing on earth ftill keeps up hell.
Nor have we yet quite purg'd the Chriftian land ;
Still idols here, like calves at Bethel, ftand.
And though Pan's death [f] long fince all oracles
  broke,
Yet ftill in rhyme the fiend Apollo fpoke :

[f] —*Pan's death*] Alluding to the famous ftory in
Plutarch's Dialogue *concerning the filence of the pagan
oracles*, and the ufe made of that ftory by Eufebius and
others; whence it became the general opinion of the
learned, in our author's days, that, by the death of
the GREAT PAN, was meant the crucifixion of our
Saviour.

         Nay

Nay with the worſt of heathen dotage we
(Vain men !) the monſter woman deify ;
Find ſtars, and tie our fates there, in a face,
And Paradiſe in them, by whom we loſt it, place.
What different faults corrupt our Muſes thus !
Wanton as girls ; as old wives, fabulous !

   Thy ſpotleſs Muſe, like Mary, did contain
The boundleſs Godhead ; ſhe did well diſdain
That her eternal verſe employ'd ſhould be
On a leſs ſubjeЄt than eternity ;
And for a ſacred miſtreſs ſcorn'd to take,
But her, whom God himſelf ſcorn'd not his ſpouſe
    to make.
It (in a kind) her miracle did do ;
A fruitful mother was, and virgin too.
   How well (bleſt ſwan) did fate contrive thy
    death [g] ;
And made thee render up thy tuneful breath
In thy great miſtreſs' arms ! thou moſt divine
And richeſt offering of Loretto's ſhrine !
Where, like ſome holy ſacrifice, t'expire,
A fever burns thee, and love lights the fire.
Angels (they ſay) brought the fam'd chapel there,
And bore the ſacred load in triumph through the
   air.

[g] Mr. Craſhaw died of a fever at Loretto, being
newly choſen canon of that church. COWLEY.

'Tis furer much, they brought thee there; and they,
And thou, their charge, went finging all the way.
  Pardon, my mother church, if I confent
That angels led him, when from thee he went;
For even in error fure no danger is,
When join'd with fo much piety as his.
Ah, mighty God, with fhame I fpeak't, and grief,
Ah that our greateft faults were in belief!
And our weak reafon were ev'n weaker yet,
Rather than thus our wills too ftrong for it!
His faith, perhaps, in fome nice tenets might
Be wrong; his life, I'm fure, was in the right [*b*].
And I myfelf a catholic will be,
So far at leaft, great faint, to pray to thee.
  Hail, bard triumphant [*i*]! and fome care beftow
On us, the poets militant below!

[*b*] Hence the famous lines of Mr. Pope, which
have given fuch fcandal to fome, and triumph to others,
only becaufe both parties have been more in hafte to
apply than underftand them —

  " For modes of faith let gracelefs zealots fight,
  " His can't be wrong, whofe life is in the right."

  [*i*] *Hail, bard triumphant!*] Hence the apoftrophe of
Mr. Pope, but not fo happily applied, as here —
  " Hail, bards triumphant, born in happier days!"
                              Effay on Crit. ver. 189.

                              Oppos'd

Oppos'd by our old enemy, adverfe chance,
Attack'd by envy, and by ignorance,
Enchain'd by beauty, tortur'd by defires,
Expos'd by tyrant-love to favage beafts and fires [*k*].
Thou from low earth in nobler flames didft rife,
And, like Elijah, mount alive the fkjes.
Elifha-like (but with a wifh much lefs,
More fit thy greatnefs, and my littlenefs)
Lo here I beg (I whom thou once didft prove
So humble to efteem, fo good to love)
Not that thy fpirit might on me doubled be,
I afk but half thy mighty fpirit for me.
And, when my Mufe foars with fo ftrong a wing,
'Twill learn of things divine, and firft of thee, to
    fing.

IX.

Imitation of MARTIAL [*l*], Lib. V. Ep. xxi.

  " S I tecum mihi, care Martialis,
  " Securis liceat frui diebus ;

[*k*] Expos'd by tyrant-love to *favage beafts and fires.*]
As the primitive Chriftians were, by the *tyrant-bate* of
their pagan perfecutors. ANON.
  [*l*] Ed. Maittaire, Lond. 1716.
      K 4   " Si

" Si difponere tempus otiofum,
" Et veræ pariter vacare vitæ :
" Nec nos atria, nec domos potentum,
" Nec lites tetricas, forúmque trifte
" Noffemus, nec imagines fuperbas :
" Sed geftatio, fabulæ, libelli,
" Campus, porticus, umbra, virgo, thermæ;
" Hæc effent loca femper, hi labores.
" Nunc vivit fibi neuter, heu, bonófque
" Soles effugere, atque abire fentit;
" Qui nobis pereunt, & imputantur.
" Quifquam vivere cùm fciat, moratur?"

IF, deareft friend, it my good fate might be
  T' enjoy at once a quiet life and thee;
If we for happinefs could leifure find [*m*],
And wandering time into a method bind;
We fhould not fure the great man's favour need,
Nor on long hopes, the court's thin diet, feed.

  [*m*] *If we for happinefs could leifure find*] An exquifite
line! of which Mr. Gray felt, and has expreffed,
all the pathos, when, in his Hymn to Adverfity, he
faid—
    " Scar'd at thy frown terrific, fly
    " Self-pleafing Folly's idle brood,
    " Wild Laughter, Noife, and thoughtlefs Joy,
    " *And leave us leifure to be good.*"   ANON.

                                              We

We ſhould not patience find, daily to hear
The calumnies, and flatteries, ſpoken there.
We ſhould not a lord's table humbly uſe,
Or talk, in ladies chambers, love and news;
But books and wiſe diſcourſe, gardens and fields,
And all the joys that unmix'd nature yields. ,
Thick ſummer ſhades, where winter ſtill does lye;
Bright winter fires, that ſummer's part ſupply.
Sleep, not controll'd by cares, confin'd to night;
Or bound in any rule, but appetite. .....
Free, but not ſavage or ungracious mirth;
Rich wines, to give it quick and eaſy birth.
A few companions, which ourſelves ſhould chuſe,
A gentle miſtreſs, and a gentler Muſe.
Such, deareſt friend, ſuch, without doubt, ſhould
      be
Our place, our buſineſs, and our company.
Now to himſelf, alas, does neither live,
But ſees good ſuns, of which we are to give
A ſtrict account, ſet and march thick away:
Knows a man how to live, and does he ſtay?

X.

ANACREONTICS [n]:

OR,

Some Copies of Verses translated Paraphrasti-
cally out of ANACREON.

I.

LOVE.

I'LL sing of heroes, and of kings;
 In mighty numbers, mighty things.
Begin, my Muse; but lo, the strings
To my great song rebellious prove;
The strings will sound of nought, but love.
I broke them all, and put on new;
'Tis this, or nothing sure, will do.
These sure (said I) will me obey;
These sure heroic notes will play.

[n] These *Anacreontics* shew, that the author
wanted neither ease of expression nor the grace of
numbers, when he followed the bent of his own taste
and genius.

Straight

Straight I began with thundering Jove,
And all th' immortal pow'rs, but love.
Love fmil'd ; and from my enfeebled lyre
Came gentle airs, fuch as infpire
Melting love, and foft defire.
Farewel, then, heroes, farewel kings,
And mighty numbers, mighty things ;
Love tunes my heart juft to my ftrings.

II.

DRINKING.

THE thirfty earth foaks up the rain,
And drinks, and gapes for drink again.
The plants fuck in the earth, and are,
With conftant drinking, frefh and fair.
The fea itfelf, which, one would think,
Should have but little need of drink,
Drinks ten thoufand rivers up,
So fill'd, that they o'erflow the cup.
The bufy fun (and one would guefs,
By's drunken fiery face, no lefs)
Drinks up the fea ; and when he'as done,
The moon and ftars drink up the fun.
They drink and dance by their own light,
They drink and revel all the night.

Nothing

Nothing in nature's fober found,
But an eternal health goes round.
Fill up the bowl then, fill it high,
Fill all the glaffes there : for why
Should every creature drink, but I,
Why, man of morals, tell me why?

III.

BEAUTY.

LIBERAL nature did difpenfe
To all things arms for their defence ;
And fome fhe arms with finewy force,
And fome, with fwiftnefs in the courfe ;
Some, with hard hoofs, or forked claws,
And fome, with horns, or tufked jaws ;
And fome with fcales, and fome with wings,
And fome with teeth, and fome with ftings.
Wifdom to man fhe did afford,
Wifdom for fhield, and wit for fword.
What to beauteous woman-kind,
What arms, what armour, has fhe affign'd ?
Beauty is both ; for with the fair
What arms, what armour, can compare ?
What fteel, what gold, or diamond,
More impaffible is found ?

And

And yet what flame, what lightning, e'er
So great an active force did bear ?
They are all weapon; and they dart,
Like porcupines, from every part.
Who can, alas, their ftrength exprefs,
Arm'd, when they themfelves undrefs,
Cap-a-pee with nakednefs ?

IV.

THE DUEL.

YES, I will love then, I will love:
I will not now love's rebel prove,
Though I was once his enemy;
Though, ill-advis'd and ftubborn, I
Did to the combat him defy.
An helmet, fpear, and mighty fhield,
Like fome new Ajax, I did wield.
Love in one hand his bow did take,
In th' other hand a dart did fhake.
But yet in vain the dart did throw,
In vain he often drew the bow.
So well my armour did refift,
So oft by flight the blow I mifs'd.
But, when I thought all danger paft,
His quiver emptied quite at laft,

Inftead

Inſtead of arrow, or of dart,
He ſhot himſelf into my heart.
The living and the killing arrow
Ran through the ſkin, the fleſh, the blood,
And broke the bones, and ſcorch'd the marrow;
No trench or work of life withſtood.
In vain. I now the walls maintain,
I ſet out guards and ſcouts in vain,
Since th' enemy does within remain.
In vain a breaſt-plate now I wear,
Since in my breaſt the foe I bear.
In vain my feet their ſwiftneſs try;
For from the body can they fly ?

V.

AGE.

OFT am I by the women told,
Poor Anacreon, thou grow'ſt old :
Look, how thy hairs are falling all;
Poor Anacreon, how they fall !
Whether I grow old or no,
By th' effects I do not know.
This I know, without being told,
'Tis time to live, if I grow old;

'Tis

'Tis time fhort pleafures now to take,
Of little life the beft to make,
And manage wifely the laft ftake.

VI.

THE ACCOUNT.

WHEN all the ftars are by thee told
(The endlefs fums of heavenly gold);
Or, when the hairs are reckon'd all;
From fickly autumn's head that fall,
Or, when the drops that make the fea,
Whilft all her fands thy counters be;
Thou then, and thou alone, may'ft prove
Th' arithmetician of my love.
An hundred loves at Athens fcore,
At Corinth write an hundred more:
Fair Corinth does fuch beauties bear,
So few is an efcaping there [o].
Write then at Chios feventy-three;
Write then at Lefbos (let me fee)
Write me at Lefbos ninety down,
Full ninety loves, and half a one.

[o] — *an efcaping there.*] A ftroke of moral fatire, flid
in, on that city, fo infamous for its brothelry. The poet
is fage, even in thefe mad Anacreontics.

And

And next to thefe let me prefent
The fair Ionian regiment.
And next the Carian company,
Five hundred both effectively [*p*].
Three hundred more at Rhodes and Crete;
Three hundred 'tis, I'm fure, complete;
For arms at Crete each face does bear,
And every eye's an archer there.
Go on; this ftop why doft thou make?
Thou think'ft, perhaps, that I miftake.
Seems this to thee too great a fum?
Why, many thoufands are to come;
The mighty Xerxes could not boaft
Such different nations in his hoft.
On; for my love, if thou be'ft weary,
Muft find fome better fecretary.
I have not yet my Perfian told,
Nor yet my Syrian loves enroll'd,
Nor Indian, nor Arabian;
Nor Cyprian loves, nor African;
Nor Scythian, nor Italian flames;
There's a whole map behind of names:
Of gentle loves i'th' temperate zone,
And cold ones in the frigid zone;

[*p*] — *effectively*.] The term in ufe with military men
(and therefore humouroufly affected here) for *completely*.

Cold

Cold frozen loves, with which I pine,
And parched loves, beneath the line;

VII.

GOLD.

A MIGHTY pain to love it is,
And 'tis a pain that pain to miss.
But of all pains the greatest pain
It is to love, but love in vain.
Virtue now, nor noble blood,
Nor wit by love is understood,
Gold alone does passion move,
Gold monopolizes love!
A curse on her, and on the man
Who this traffic first began!
A curse on him who found the ore!
A curse on him who digg'd the store!
A curse on him who did refine it!
A curse on him who first did coin it!
A curse, all curses else above,
On him, who us'd it first in love;
Gold begets in brethren hate,
Gold, in families debate;
Gold, does friendships separate,
Gold, does civil wars create.

Theſe

Thefe the fmalleft harms of it!
Gold, alas, does love beget.

VIII.

THE EPICURE.

FILL the bowl with rofy wine,
Around our temples rofes twine;
And let us chearfully awhile,
Like the wine and rofes, fmile.
Crown'd with rofes, we contemn
Gyges' wealthy diadem.
To-day is our's; what do we fear?
To-day is our's; we have it here.
Let's treat it kindly, that it may
Wifh, at leaft, with us to ftay.
Let's banifh bufinefs, banifh forrow;
To the gods, belongs to-morrow.

IX.

ANOTHER.

UNDERNEATH this myrtle fhade,
On flowery beds fupinely laid,
With odorous oils my head o'er-flowing,
And around it rofes growing,

What

What fhould I do but drink away
The heat and troubles of the day?
In this more than kingly ftate,
Love himfelf fhall on me wait.
Fill to me, love, nay, fill it up;
And mingled caft into the cup,
Wit, and mirth, and noble fires,
Vigorous health, and gay defires.
The wheel of life no lefs will ftay
In a fmooth, than rugged way.
Since it equally does flee,
Let the motion pleafant be.
Why do we precious ointments fhower,
Nobler wines why do we pour,
Beauteous flowers why do we fpread,
Upon the monuments of the dead?
Nothing they but duft can fhow,
Or bones, that haften to be fo.
Crown me with rofes whilft I live,
Now your wines and ointments give.
After death I nothing crave,
Let me alive my pleafures have;
All are Stoics in the grave.

X. THE

X.

THE GRASSHOPPER.

HAPPY infect, what can be,
In happinefs, compar'd to thee ?
Fed with nourifhment divine,
The dewy morning's gentle wine !
Nature waits upon thee ftill,
And thy verdant cup does fill,
'Tis fill'd, wherever thou doft tread,
Nature's felf's thy Ganymed.
Thou doft drink, and dance, and fing;
Happier, than the happieft king !
All the fields, which thou doft fee,
All the plants, belong to thee,
All that fummer hours produce,
Fertile made. with early juice.
Man for thee does fow and plow :
Farmer he, and landlord thou !
Thou doft innocently joy,
Nor does thy luxury deftroy;
The fhepherd gladly heareth thee,
More harmonious than he.
Thee, country hinds with gladnefs hear,
Prophet of the ripen'd year !

Thee,

Thee, Phœbus loves, and does infpire;
Phœbus is himfelf thy fire.
To thee, of all things upon earth,
Life is no longer than thy mirth.
Happy infect, happy thou
Doft neither age nor winter know.
But, when thou'ft drunk, and d a n c 'd, and fu
Thy fill, the flowery leaves among,
(Voluptuous, and wife, with all,
Epicurean animal !)
Sated with thy fummer feaft,
Thou retir'ft to endlefs reft.

XI.

THE SWALLOW.

FOOLISH prater, what doft thou
So early at my window do,
With thy tunelefs ferenade ?
Well 't had been, had Tereus made
Thee, as dumb, as Philomel;
There his knife had done but well.
In thy undifcover'd neft
Thou doft all the winter reft,
And dreameft o'er thy fummer joys,
Free from the ftormy feafon's noife;

Free

Free from th' ill thou'ft done to me :
Who difturbs, or feeks out thee ?
Hadft thou all the charming notes
Of the wood's poetic throats,
All thy art could never pay
What thou'ft ta'en from me away :
Cruel bird, thou'ft ta'en away
A dream out of my arms to-day,
A dream, that ne'er muft equal'd be
By all that waking eyes may fee,
Thou, this damage to repair,
Nothing half fo fweet or fair,
Nothing half fo good can'ft bring,
Though men fay, *Thou bring'ft the fpring.*

****

XII.

ELEGY UPON ANACREON,

who was choaked by a GRAPE-STONE.

Spoken by the God of Love.

HOW fhall I lament thine end,
My beft fervant, and my friend ?
Nay, and, if from a deity
So much deified as I,

It found not too profane and odd,
Oh my mafter, and my god!
For 'tis true, moft mighty poet,
(Though I like not, men fhould know it)
I am in naked nature lefs,
Lefs by much, than in thy drefs.
All thy verfe is fofter far
Than the downy feathers are
Of my wings, or of my arrows,
Of my mother's doves, or fparrows.
Sweet, as lovers frefheft kiffes;
Or, their riper following bliffes;
Graceful, cleanly, fmooth, and round,
All with Venus' girdle bound;
And thy life was all the while
Kind and gentle, as thy ftyle.
The fmooth-pac'd hours of ev'ry day
Glided numeroufly away.
Like thy verfe, each hour did pafs;
Sweet and fhort, like that it was.

Some do but their youth allow me,
Juft what they, by nature owe me;
The time, that's mine, and not their own,
The certain tribute of my crown.
When they grow old, they grow to be
Too bufy, or too wife, for me.

L 4

Thou

Thou wert wifer, and didft know,
None too wife for love can grow;
Love was with thy life entwin'd
Clofe, as heat with fire is join'd,
A powerful brand prefcrib'd the date
Of thine, like Meleager's fate.
Th' antiperiftafis [*q*] of age
More enflam'd thy amorous rage;
Thy filver hairs yielded me more,
Than even golden curls, before.

Had I the power of creation,
As I have of generation,
Where I the matter muft obey,
And cannot work plate out of clay;
My creatures fhould be all like thee,
'Tis thou fhould their idea be.

[*q*] *Antiperiftafis*] This hard word only means, *com-
preffion*. The word is ufed by naturalifts to exprefs the
power, which one quality has, *by preffing on all fides*, to
augment its contrary: as here the *cold*, with which old
age is environed, increafes heat. He expreffes this
quaint idea more plainly in two verfes of THE MIS-
TRESS (left out in this collection), where he fays—
"Flames their moft vigorous heat do hold,
"And pureft light, if *compafs'd round with cold.*"
                                            The Requeft, St. 3.

                                                    They,

They, like thee, ſhould throughly hate
Buſineſs, honour, title, ſtate.
Other wealth they ſhould not know,
But what my living mines beſtow ;
The pomp of kings they ſhould confeſs
At their crownings to be leſs
Than a lover's humbleſt guiſe,
When at his miſtreſs' feet he lies.
Rumour they no more ſhould mind
Than men ſafe-landed do, the wind ;
Wiſdom itſelf they ſhould not hear,
When it preſumes to be ſevere.
Beauty alone they ſhould admire ;
Nor look at fortune's vain attire,
Nor aſk what parents it can ſhew ;
With dead, or old, t' has nought to do,
They ſhould not love yet all, or any,
But very much, and very many.
All their life ſhould gilded be
With mirth, and wit, and gaiety,
Well remembering, and applying
The neceſſity of dying,
Their chearful heads ſhould always wear
All that crowns the flowery year.
They ſhould always laugh, and ſing,
And dance, and ſtrike th' harmonious ſtring.

I   Verſe

Verfe fhould from their tongue fo flow,
As if it in the mouth did grow,
As fwiftly anfwering their command,
As tunes obey the artful hand.
And, whilft I do thus difcover
Th' ingredients of a happy lover,
'Tis, my Anacreon, for thy fake
I of the grape no mention make.
  Till my Anacreon by thee fell,
Curfed plant, I lov'd thee well.
And 'twas oft my wanton ufe,
To dip my arrows in thy juice.
Curfed plant, 'tis true, I fee,
The old report that goes of thee,
That with giants blood the earth
Stain'd and poifon'd gave thee birth,
And now thou wreak'ft thy ancient fpight
On men, in whom the gods delight,
Thy patron Bacchus, 'tis no wonder,
Was brought forth in flames and thunder;
In rage, in quarrels, and in fights,
Worfe than his tigers, he delights :
In all our heaven I think there be [r]
No fuch ill-natur'd god as he.

  [r] — *I think there be*] " I think, Crab, my dog *be*
the foureft-natured dog that lives." [*Shakefp. Two Gent.*

Thou pretendeſt, traiterous wine,
To be the Muſes friend and mine.
With love and wit thou doſt begin,
Falſe fires, alas, to draw us in,
Which, if our courſe we by them keep,
Miſguide to madneſs, or to ſleep.
Sleep were well; thou'ſt learnt a way
To death itſelf now to betray.

It grieves me, when I ſee what fate
Does on the beſt of mankind wait.
Poets, or lovers, let them be,
'Tis neither love nor poeſy
Can arm againſt death's ſmalleſt dart
The poet's ' ead, or lover's heart.
But, when their life, in its decline,
Touches th' inevitable line,
All the world's mortal to 'em then,
And wine is aconite to men.

of *Verona*, *A.* 11. *S.* 3.] *Be*, for *am* or *is*, was origi-
nally the miſtake of one *mode* for another. It, afterwards, grew into credit; and ſeemed to take an air of
conſiſtency and regularity, when ſomebody had be-
thought himſelf to uſe, *be'ſt*, in the Second Perſon,
for *art*. Hence, what grammarians call, the *double
form* in the Indicative Preſent of the Auxiliary, *to be*.
It is, now, deſervedly exploded.

Nay,

Nay, in death's hand, the grape-ftone proves
As ftrong, as thunder is in Jove's.

XI.

THE CHRONICLE.

A BALLAD [s].

1.

MARGARITA firft poffefs'd,
    If I remember well, my breaft,
    Margarita, firft of all;
But, when a while the wanton maid
With my reftlefs heart had play'd,
    Martha took the flying ball.

2.

Martha foon did it refign
    To the beauteous Catharine.

[s] This agreeable Ballad has had juftice done to it.
Nothing is more famous, even in our days, than
Cowley's *miftreffes.*

                     Beauteous

Beauteous Catharine gave place
(Though loth and angry fhe to part
With the poffeffion of my heart)
    To Elifa's conquering face.

3.

Elifa till this hour might reign,
    Had fhe not evil counfels ta'en:
    Fundamental laws fhe broke,
And ftill new favourites fhe chofe,
Till up in arms my paffions rofe,
    And caft away her yoke.

4.

Mary then and gentle Anne
    Both to reign at once began;
    Alternately they fway'd:
And fometimes Mary was the fair,
And fometimes Anne the crown did wear,
    And fometimes both I' obey'd.

5.

Another Mary then arofe,
    And did rigorous laws impofe:
    A mighty tyrant, fhe!
Long, alas, fhould I have been
Under that iron-fcepter'd queen,
    Had not Rebecca fet me free.

6. When

6.

When fair Rebecca set me free,
    'Twas then a golden time with me;
    But soon those pleasures fled;
For the gracious princess dy'd
In her youth and beauty's pride,
    And Judith reigned in her stead.

7.

One month, three days, and half an hour,
    Judith held the sovereign power;
    Wondrous beautiful her face;
But so weak and small her wit,
That she to govern was unfit,
    And so Susanna took her place.

8.

But, when Isabella came,
    Arm'd with a resistless flame,
    And th' artillery of her eye;
Whilst she proudly march'd about
Greater conquests to find out,
    She beat out Susan by the bye.

9.

But in her place I then obey'd
    Black-ey'd Bess, her viceroy-maid,

To

To whom enfu'd a vacancy.
Thoufand worfe paffions then poffefs'd
The interregnum of my breaft :
  Blefs me from fuch an anarchy !

10.

Gentle Henrietta than [*t*],
    And a third Mary next began ;
    Then Joan, and Jane, and Audria,
And then a pretty Thomafine,
And then another Katharine,
    And then a long *et cætera.*

11.

But fhould I now to you relate,
    The ftrength and riches of their ftate,
    The powder, patches, and the pins,
The ribbands, jewels, and the rings,
The lace, the paint, and warlike things,
    That make up all their magazines :

[*t*] —*than*] So fpelt (as many other words in thefe
poems are) for the fake of the rhyme. He had learned
this art, or licence rather, from Spenfer, who practifed
it very frequently. But he might have learned better
things from our old poet, if this early favourite of his
youth had been taken for the model of his riper
age.

12. If

12.

If I fhould tell the politic arts
　　To take and keep mens hearts;
　　The letters, embaffies, and fpies,
The frowns, and fmiles, and flatteries,
The quarrels, tears, and perjuries,
　　Numberlefs, namelefs myfteries !

13.

And all the little lime-twigs laid
　　By Machiavel, the waiting-maid;
　　I more voluminous fhould grow
(Chiefly, if I like them fhould tell
All change of weathers [*u*] that befell)
　　Than Holinfhead or Stow.

14.

But I will briefer with them be,
　　Since few of them were long with me.
　　An higher and a nobler ftrain
My prefent emperefs does claim,
Heleonora, *firft o'th' name* ; · ·
　　Whom *God grant long to reign !*

　　[*u*] — *change of weathers*] His brilliant wit, for
once, is well placed.

XII. ODE.

XII.

O D E.

ACME and SEPTIMIUS:
Out of CATULLUS.

WHILST on Septimius' panting breaſt,
(Meaning nothing leſs than reſt)
Acme lean'd her loving head,
Thus the pleas'd Septimius ſaid;

My deareſt Acme, if I be
Once alive, and love not thee
With a paſſion far above
All that e'er was called love,
In a Libyan deſert may
I become ſome lion's prey;
Let him, Acme, let him tear
My breaſt, when Acme is not there.

The god of love, who ſtood to hear him,
(The god of love was always near him)

Pleas'd and tickled with the found,
Sneez'd aloud: and all around
The little loves, that waited by,
Bow'd, and blefs'd the augury.
Acme, inflam'd with what he faid,
Rear'd her gently-bending head,
And, her purple mouth, with joy
Stretching to the delicious boy,
Twice (and twice could fcarce fuffice)
She kifs'd his drunken, rowling eyes.

My little life, my all (faid fhe),
So may we ever fervants be
To this beft god, and ne'er retain
Our hated liberty again,
So may thy paffion laft for me,
As I a paffion have for thee,
Greater and fiercer much than can
Be conceiv'd by thee, a man.
Into my marrow is it gone,
Fix'd and fettled in the bone;
It reigns not only in my heart,
But runs, like life through ev'ry part.
She fpoke; the god of love, aloud,
Sneez'd again; and all the crowd
Of little loves, that waited by,
Bow'd, and blefs'd the augury.

This

This good omen thus from heaven,
Like a happy fignal, given,
Their loves and lives (all four) embrace,
And hand in hand run all the race.
To poor Septimius (who did now
Nothing elfe but Acme grow)
Acme's bofom was alone
The whole world's imperial throne;
And to faithful Acme's mind
Septimius was all human kind.

If the gods would pleafe to be
But advis'd for once by me,
I'd advife them, when them fpy
Any illuftrious piety,
To reward her, if it be fhe;
To reward him, if it be he;
With fuch a hufband, fuch a wife [w],
With Acme's and Septimius' life.

[w] —*fuch a* hufband, *fuch a* wife] It is to be obferved, to the honour of our author's morals, and good
tafte, that, by this little deviation from his original, he
has converted a loofe love-poem into a fober epithala-
mium. We have all the grace, and, what is more, all
the warmth of Catullus, without his indecency.

XIII. THE

XIII.

THE PRAISE OF PINDAR [*x*].

AN ODE:

In Imitation of HORACE, 4 Od. ii.

I.

PINDAR is imitable by none;
    The phœnix Pindar is a vaſt ſpecies alone.
Whoe'er, but Dædalus, with waxen wings could fly,
And neither ſink too low, nor ſoar too high?
    What could he, who follow'd, claim,
But of vain boldneſs the unhappy fame,
    And, by his fall, a ſea to name?

[*x*] *The praiſe of Pindar.*] This, and the three following odes are in the number of thoſe, which Mr.
Cowley calls, *Pindaric*: an exquiſite ſort of poetry, to
which his *ſtyle* was very ill ſuited; being, for the moſt
part, careleſs, and ſometimes, affectedly vulgar.—The
ideas, in this ode, are from Horace; but the ſpirit and
expreſſion, are the writer's own.

I   Pindar's

Pindar's unnavigable fong,
Like a fwoln flood from fome fteep mountain, pours
    along ;
The ocean meets with fuch a voice
From his enlarged mouth, as drowns the ocean's
    noife.

2.

So Pindar does new words and figures roul
Down his impetuous dithyrambic tide,
    Which in no channel deigns t'abide,
    Which neither banks nor dikes controul.
    Whether th' immortal gods he fings
    In a no lefs immortal ftrain ;
Or the great acts of god-defcended kings,
Who in his numbers ftill furvive and reign.
    Each rich embroider'd line,
  Which their triumphant brows around,
    By his facred hand, is bound,
Does all their ftarry diadems outfhine.

3.

Whether at Pifa's race he pleafe
To carve in polifh'd verfe the conquerors images :
Whether the fwift, the fkilful, or the ftrong,
Be crowned in his nimble, artful, vigorous fong :
    Whether

Whether fome brave young man's untimely fate,
In words worth dying for, he celebrate,
　　Such mournful, and fuch pleafing words,
As joy t'his mother's and his miftrefs' grief affords:
　　He bids him live and grow in fame,
　　Among the ftars he fticks his name [y];
The grave can but the drofs of him devour;
So fmall is death's, fo great the poet's, power.

　　　　　　　　　4.

Lo, how th' obfequious wind, and fwelling air,
　　The Theban fwan [z] does upwards bear
Into the walks of clouds, where he does play,
And with extended wings open his liquid way,
　　Whilft, alas, my tim'rous Mufe
　　Unambitious tracks purfues;

　　[y] *Among the ftars he fticks his name*]
" Stellis inferere, et concilio Jovis." Hor. 3 Od.
xxv. 6. COWLEY.
[z] *The Theban fwan*] Mr. Gray calls him, *the Theban
eagle*; but the imagery of both poets is much the fame.
　　　　　　—— " tho' he inherit
　　" Nor the pride, nor ample pinion,
　　　" That the Theban eagle bear,
　　" Sailing with fupreme dominion
　　　" Thro' the azure deep of air." Progrefs of Poetry.
　　　　　　　　　　　　　　　Does,

Does, with weak unballaſt wings,
About the moſſy brooks and ſprings;
About the trees new-bloſſom'd heads,
About the gardens painted beds,
About the fields and flowery meads,
And all inferior beauteous things,
 Like the laborious bee,
For little drops of honey flee [a],
And therewith humble ſweets contents her induſtry.

XIV.

Ι. RUTUS [b].

AN ODE.

I.

EXCELLENT Brutus, of all human race
 The beſt, till nature was improv'd by grace,

[a]—flee] The proper word had been *fly*, if the rhyme would have given leave. To *flee*, is properly to *move with ſpeed out of the way of danger*; to *fly*, to *move with ſpeed on* WINGS.

[b] The ſubject of this ode ſeems to have been choſen by the poet, for the ſake of venting his indig-

Till

Till men above themſelves faith raiſed more,
    Than reaſon above beaſts, before.
Virtue was thy life's centre, and from thence
Did ſilently and conſtantly diſpenſe
    The gentle vigorous influence
To all the wide and fair circumference :
And all the parts upon it lean'd ſo eaſily,
Obey'd the mighty force ſo willingly,

nation againſt Cromwell.—It has been generally ſuppoſ-
ed, that Mr. Cowley had no ear for harmony, and even
no táſte of elegant expreſſion. And one ſhould be apt to
think ſo, from his untuned verſe and rugged ſtyle : but
the caſe was only this : Donne and Jonſon were the favourite poets of the time, and therefore thuſmodels, on
which our poet was ambitious to form hiɾſelf. But unhappily theſe poets *affected* harſh numbers and uncooth
expreſſion ; and what they affected, eaſily came to be
looked upon as *beauties*.   Even Milton himſelf, in his
younger days, fell into this deluſion. [See his poem on
Shakeſpear.]   But the vigour of his genius, or, perhaps,
his courſe of life, which led him out of the high-road of
faſhion, enabled him, in good time, to break through
the ſnare of—*exemplar vitiis imitabile.* The court, which
had worſe things to anſwer for, kept poor Cowley eter-
nally in it. *He forſook the converſation* (ſays Dr. Sprat,
who deſigned him a compliment in the obſervation),
but never THE LANGUAGE OF THE COURT.

                                                    That

That none could difcord or diforder fee
    In all their contrariety.
Each had his motion natural and free,
And the whole no more mov'd, than the whole
    world could be.

2.

From the ftrict rule fome think that thou didft
    fwerve
(Miftaken honeft men) in Cæfar's blood :
What mercy could the tyrant's life deferve
From him, who kill'd himfelf, rather than ferve ?
Th' heroic exaltations of good
    Are fo far from underftood,
We count them vice : alas, our fight's fo ill,
That things, which fwifteft move, feem to ftand ftill.
We look not upon virtue in her height,
On her fupreme idea, brave and bright,
    In the original light ;
    But as her beams reflected pafs
Through our own nature, or ill cuftom's glafs :
    And 'tis no wonder fo,
    If, with dejected eye,
    In ftanding pools we feek the fky,
That ftars, fo high above, fhould feem to us below.

3. Can

3.

Can we ſtand by, and ſee
Our mother robb'd, and bound, and raviſh'd be,
 Yet not to her aſſiſtance ſtir,
Pleas'd with the ſtrength and beauty of the ra-
 viſher [c] ?
 Or, ſhall we fear to kill him, if before
 The cancel'd name of friend he bore ?
 Ingrateful Brutus do they call ?
Ingrateful Cæſar, who could Rome enthral !
In act more barbarous and unnatural
(In th' exact balance of true virtue tried)
Than his ſucceſſor Nero's parricide !

 There's none, but Brutus, could deſerve
 That all men elſe ſhould wiſh to ſerve,

[c] This is well put. But *piety to the mother* muſt not
extinguiſh all regard for the mother's *ſons*. Nothing con-
tributed ſo much, as the aſſaſſination of the firſt Cæſar,
to bring on all thoſe tragedies, with which the gloomy
and unappeaſable jealouſy of his ſucceſſors, afterwards,
filled the Roman annals. The queſtion is not, what Cæſar deſerved, but what the true intereſt of the Roman people required. For in theſe caſes, as Macbeth well obſerves,
 —— " we but teach
 " Bloody inſtructions, which, being taught, return
 " To plague th' inventor"—— Act I. S. viii.

 And

And Cæfar's ufurp'd place to him fhould proffer;
None can deferve 't, but he, who would refufe
    the offer.

4.

Ill fate affum'd a body, thee t' affright,
And wrapt itfelf i'th' terrors of the night,
I'll meet thee at Philippi, faid the fpright:
    I'll meet thee there, faidft thou,
    With fuch a voice, and fuch a brow,
As put the trembling ghoft to fudden flight;
    It vanifh'd, as a taper's light
    Goes out, when fpirits appear in fight.
One would have thought, 't had heard the morn-
    ing crow,
    Or feen her well-appointed ftar
Come marching up the eaftern hill afar [d].
Nor durft it in Philippi's field appear,
    But unfeen attack'd thee there.
Had it prefum'd in any fhape thee to oppofe,
Thou wouldft have forc'd it back upon thy foes:

[d] —*eaftern hill afar.*]
" Till down the eaftern cliffs afar,
" Hyperion's march they fpy, and glitt'ring fhafts of
    " war."   Mr. Gray.

                            Or

Or flain 't, like Cæfar, though it be
A conqueror, and a monarch, mightier far than he,

5.

What joy can human things to us afford,
When we fee perifh thus, by odd events,
  Ill men, and wretched accidents,
The beft caufe, and beft man that ever drew a fword?
   When we fee
The falfe Octavius, and wild Antony,
  God-like Brutus, conquer thee?
What can we fay, but thine own tragic word,
That virtue, which had worfhip'd been by thee
As the moft folid good, and greateft deity,
  By this fatal proof became
  An idol only, and a name?
 Hold, noble Brutus, and reftrain
The bold voice of thy generous difdain :
  Thefe mighty gulphs are yet
Too deep for all thy judgement and thy wit.
The time's fet forth already, which fhall quell
Stiff reafon, when it offers to rebell ;
  Which thefe great fecrets fhall unfeal,
  And new philofophies reveal.

      A few

A few years more, fo foon hadft thou not died,
Would have confounded human virtue's pride,
   And fhew'd thee a God crucified.

XV.

To Mr. Hobbes [*e*].

I.

Vast bodies of philofophy
   I oft have feen, and read ;
     But all are bodies dead,
   Or bodies by art fafhioned :
I never yet the living foul could fee,
     But in thy books, and thee.
    'Tis only God can know
Whether the fair idea thou doft fhow
Agree intirely with his own, or no.

[*e*] Mr. Hobbes was, at this time, the philofopher in
fafhion : and Mr. Cowley fpeaks the fafhionable, rather
than his own fenfe of him; as appears from the exag-
gerated ftrain of his panegyric. However, he does but
juftice to the vigour of his fenfe, and the manly elegance
of his ftyle : for the *latter* of which qualities, chiefly,
his philofophic writings are now valuable.

                          This

This I dare boldly tell,
'Tis so like truth, 'twill serve our turn as well [*f*].
Just, as in nature, thy proportions be,
As full of concord, their variety;
As firm the parts upon their centre rest;
And all so solid are, that they at least,
As much as nature, emptiness detest.

2.

Long did the mighty Stagirite retain [*g*]
The universal intellectual reign,
Saw his own country's short-liv'd leopard slain [*h*];
The stronger Roman-eagle did outfly [*i*],
Oftner renewed his age, and saw that die;

[*f*]   *This I dare boldly tell,*
'Tis so like truth, 'twill serve our turn as well.] The
writer, indeed, is a poet: but this was rather *too boldly*
said.

[*g*] Aristotle; so called from the town of Stagira,
where he was born, situated near the bay of Strymon in
Macedonia. COWLEY.

[*h*] Outlasted the Grecian empire, which, in the visions
of Daniel, is represented, by a leopard, with four wings
upon the back, and four heads, chap. vii. 6. COWLEY.

[*i*] Was received even beyond the bounds of the Roman empire, and out-lived it. COWLEY.

Meccha itfelf, in fpight of Mahomet, poffefs'd[*k*],
And, chas'd by a wild deluge from the Eaft,
His monarchy new planted in the Weft.
But, as in time each great imperial race
Degenerates, and gives fome new one place ;
   So did this noble empire wafte,
    Sunk by degrees from glories paft,
And in the fchool-mens hands it perifh'd quite at laft.
   Then nought but words it grew,
    And thofe all barbarous too :
  It perifh'd, and it vanifh'd there,
The life and foul, breath'd out, became but
  empty air.

[*k*] For Ariftotle's philofophy was in great efteem
among the Arabians or Saracens ; witnefs thofe many
excellent books upon him, or according to his principles,
written by Averroes, Avicenna, Avempace, and divers
others. *In fpight of Mahomet :* becaufe his law, being
adapted to the barbarous humour of thofe people he had
firft to deal withal, and aiming only at greatnefs of empire by the fword, forbids all the ftudies of learning ;
which (neverthelefs) florifhed admirably under the Sa-
racen monarchy, and continued fo, till it was extinguifh-
ed with that empire, by the inundation of the Turks,
and other nations. Meccha is the town in Arabia
where Mahomet was born. COWLEY.

3.

The fields, which anfwer'd well the ancients plough,
Spent and out-worn, return no harveſt now,
In barren age wild and unglorious lie,
  And boaſt of paſt fertility,
The poor relief of prefent poverty.
  Food and fruit we now muſt want,
   Unlefs new lands we plant.
We break up tombs with facrilegious hands ;
  Old rubbiſh we remove ;
To walk in ruins, like vain ghoſts, we love.
  And with fond divining wands [*l*]
   We fearch among the dead ·
   For treafures buried,
  Whilſt ſtill the liberal earth does hold
So many virgin mines of undifcover'd gold.

4.

The Baltic, Euxine, and the Cafpian,
And ſlender-limb'd Mediterranean [*m*],

[*l*] *Virgula divina*, or a divining wand, is a two-forked
branch of an hazel-tree, which is ufed for the finding out
either of veins, or hidden treafures, of gold or filver ;
and being carried about, bends downwards (or rather is
faid to do fo) when it comes to the place where they lye.
Cowley.
 [*m*] All the navigation of the ancients was in thefe
           Seem

Seem narrow creeks to thee, and only fit
For the poor wretched fisher-boats of wit.
Thy nobler veffel the vast ocean tries,
    And nothing fees, but feas and fkies,
    Till unknown regions it defcries,
Thou great Columbus of the golden lands of
    new philofophies.
    Thy tafk was harder much, than his;
    · For thy learn'd America is
Not only found out firft by thee,
And rudely left to future induftry ;
    But thy eloquence, and thy wit,
Has planted, peopled, built, and civiliz'd it.

5.

    I little thought before,
    (Nor, being my own felf fo poor,
    Could comprehend fo vaft a ftore)
That all the wardrobe of rich eloquence
    Could have afforded half enough,
    Of bright, of new, and lafting ftuff,
To cloathe the mighty limbs of thy gigantic
    fenfe [n].

feas; they feldom ventured into the ocean ; and when
they did, did only *littus legere*, coaft about near the
fhore. COWLEY.

    [n] The meaning is, that his notions are fo new, and

Thy folid reafon, like the fhield from heaven
    To the Trojan hero given [o],
Too ftrong to take a mark from any mortal dart,
Yet fhines with gold and gems in every part,
And wonders on it grav'd by the learn'd hand of art;
    A fhield, that gives delight
    Even to the enemies fight,
Then, when they're fure to lofe the combat by't [p].

6.

Nor can the fnow, which now cold age does fhed
    Upon thy reverend head,
Quench or allay the noble fires within ;
    But all which thou haft been,

fo great, that I did not think it had been poffible to have
found out words to exprefs them clearly; as no wardrobe can furnifh cloaths to fit a body taller and bigger
than ever any was before : for the cloaths were made
according to fome meafure that then was. COWLEY.
    [o] See the excellent defoription of this fhield, made
by Vulcan, at the requeft of Venus, for her fon Æneas,
at the end of the eighth book of the Æneid,
      —" et clypei non enarrabile textum."
whereon was graven all the Roman hiftory. COWLEY.
    [p] —to lofe the combat by't.] As not a few did, who
prefumed, with very unequal arms, to try the temper
of that *magic* fhield ; which time and common fenfe,
however, have at length difenchanted.

                              And

And all that youth can be, thou'rt yet ;
So fully ftill doft thou
Enjoy the manhood, and the bloom of wit,
And all the natural heat, but not the fever too.
So contraries on Ætna's top [*q*] confpire ;
Here hoary frofts, and by them breaks out fire [*r*].

[*q*] *So contraries on Ætna's top*] By. making *the frofts on Ætna's top* a comparifon only, and not enlarging directly on the contrary qualities of *cold* and *heat*, taken fometimes in the literal fenfe, and fometimes in the metaphorical, the poet has kept clear, in a good degree, of that *mixt wit* (as Mr. Addifon calls it), in which he fo much excelled and delighted. The *fire of Hobbes' genius*, breaking out under the *fnow of his gray hairs*, might have been fet in fo many different lights by our ingenious author, and have been worked up by him into fuch a variety of amufing contrafts, that the temperate ufe of his darling faculty, in this inftance, deferves our commendation.

[*r*] The defcription of the neighbourhood of fire and fnow, upon Ætna (but not the application of it) is imitated out of Claude. l. i. de Raptu Prof.

" Sed quamvis nimio ferveus exuberet æftu,
" Scit nivibus fervare fidem, pariterque favillis
" Durefcit glacies, tanti fecura vaporis,
" Arcano defenfa gelu, fumoque fideli
" Lambit contiguas innoxia flamma pruinas."

Where, methinks, is fomewhat of that which Seneca objects to Ovid, *Nefcivit quod benè ceffit relinquere.* When he met with a fancy that pleafed him, he could not find

N 2 A fecure

A fecure peace the faithful neighbours keep,
Th'embolden'd fnow next to the flame does fleep.
    And, if we weigh, like thee,
    Nature, and caufes, we fhall fee
    That thus it needs muft be ;
To things immortal time can do no wrong;
And that which never is to die, for ever muft be
    young.

in his heart to quit, or ever to have done with it. Ta-
citus has the like expreffion of Mount Libanus, *Præci-
puum montium Libanum, mirum dictu, tantos inter ardores
opacum fidumque nivibus* ; fhady among fuch great heats,
and faithful to the fnow ; which is too poetical for the
profe even of a romance, much more of an hiftorian.
Sil. Italic. of Ætna, l. xiv.
    " Summo cana jugo cohibet (mirabile dictu)
    " Vicinam flammis glaciem, æternoque rigore
    " Ardentes horrent fcopuli, ftat vertice celfi
    " Collis hyems, calidaque nivem tegit atra favillâ."
See likewife Seneca, Epift. 79. COWLEY.

XVI. LIFE

XVI.

LIFE AND FAME.

OH life, thou nothing's younger brother [*s*]!
So like, that one might take one for the other [*t*]!
What's fomebody, or nobody [*u*]?

[*s*] Becaufe nothing preceded it, as privation does all being; which perhaps is the fenfe of the diftinction of days in the ftory of the creation; night fignifying the privation, and day, the fubfequent being, from whence the evening is placed firft, Gen. i. 5. " And the even-" ing and the morning were the firft day." Cowley.

[*t*] *Oh life, thou nothing's younger brother !*
So like, that one might take one for the other !] i. e. *life is lefs than nothing, but, as being come of nothing, is very like it.* Mr. Cowley's poetry (as here) is often much disfigured by the double affectation of *wit* and *familiarity.* He would fay an out-of-the way thing, in a trivial man-ner.—But fuch was the court-idea, in his time, of *writing, like a gentleman.*

[*u*] Τί δὲ τίς, τί δ' ὔτις; Σκιᾶς ὄναρ ἄνθρωπ@. Pindar. *What is fomebody, or what is nobody ! Man is the dream of a fhadow.* Cowley.

In

In all the cobwebs of the fchoolmen's trade [*w*],
We no fuch nice-diftinction woven fee,
 As 'tis, to be, or, not to be.
Dream of a fhadow [*x*]! a reflection, made
From the falfe glories of the gay reflected bow[*y*],
 Is a more folid thing than thou.
Vain weak-built ifthmus [*z*], which doft proudly
  rife
  Up betwixt two eternities [*a*];

[*w*] The diftinctions of the fchoolmen may be likened
to cobwebs (I mean many of them, for fome are better
woven); either becaufe of the too much finenefs of the
work, which makes it flight, and able to catch only little
creatures; or becaufe they take not the materials from
nature, but fpin it out of themfelves. COWLEY.

[*x*] *Dream of a fhadow!*] Juftly admired by Plutarch, as a moft ingenious and expreffive hyperbole.
Vol. ii. p. 104. ed. Xyland. Par. 1624.

[*y*] The rainbow is in itfelf of no colour; thofe that
appear are but reflections of the fun's light received dif-
ferently—
 " Mille trahit varios adverfo fole colores:"
as is evident by artificial rainbows; and yet this fhadow,
this almoft nothing, makes fometimes another rainbow
(but not fo diftinct or beautiful) by reflection. COWLEY.

[*z*] Ifthmus is a neck of land that divides a peninfula
from the continent and is betwixt two feas, Γῆ ἀμφιθά-
λασσα. In which manner this narrow paffage of life
divides the paft time from the future, and is at laft
fwallowed up into eternity. COWLEY.

[*a*] *Ifthmus, —betwixt two eternities;*] A fublime idea,
           Yet

Yet canſt nor wave nor wind ſuſtain ;
But, broken and o'erwhelm'd, the endleſs oceans
    meet again.

2.

And with what rare inventions do we ſtrive,
    Ourſelves then to ſurvive ?
Wiſe, ſubtle arts, and ſuch as well befit
    That nothing man's no wit.
Some with vaſt coſtly tombs would purchaſe it,
And, by the proofs of death, pretend to live.
    Here lies the great—Falſe marble, where ?
Nothing but ſmall and ſordid duſt lies there.
Some build enormous mountain-palaces,
    The fools and architects to pleaſe :

which lay unnoticed in this ode, till Mr. Pope produced
it into obſervation —

    " Plac'd on this *iſthmus of a middle ſtate,*
    " A being darkly wiſe, and rudely great."

              Eſſ. on Man, ep. ii. 3.

Not but our philoſophical poet had his eye, alſo, on
M. Paſcal — "qu'eſt-ce que l'homme dans la nature ?
" Un neant à l'égard de l'infini, un tout à l'égard du
" neant, *un milieu entre rien et tout.* Il eſt infiniment
" éloigné des deux extrèmes ; et ſon être n'eſt moins
" diſtant du neant d'où il eſt tiré, que de l'infini où il
" eſt englouti." *Penſées,* c. xxii.

        N 4   A laſt-

A lafting life in well-hewn ftone they rear :
  So he, who on th' Egyptian fhore [b]
Was flain, fo many hundred years before,
Lives ftill (oh life, moft happy and moft dear !
Oh life, that Epicures envy to hear [c] !)
Lives in the drooping ruins of his amphitheatre.

3.

His [d] father-in-law [e] an higher place does claim
In the feraphic entity of fame [f].
  He, fince that toy, his death [g],
Does fill all mouths, and breathes in all men's breath.

[b] Pompey the great. COWLEY.
[c] An irony ; that is, " Oh life, which Epicures
" laugh at and contemn !" COWLEY.
[d] Cæfar, whofe daughter Julia was married to
Pompey; an alliance fatal to the commonwealth; which,
as Tully fays, ought never to have been made, or never
ended. COWLEY.
  [e] *His father-in-law*] This, again, is in the familiar ftyle. He might have faid, more fuitably to the
ftyle of an ode—
        " Great Cæfar's felf"——
  [f] Supernatural, intellectual, unintelligible being.
COWLEY.
  [g] —*that toy, his death*] Called a *toy*, becaufe the
play-thing of every declaimer, from that time to this,
                                            'Tis

'Tis true, the two immortal fyllables [*b*] remain,
    But, o ye learned men, explain,
    What effence, what exiftence this,
What fubftance, what fubfiftence, what hypoftafis,
    In fix poor letters is ?
In thofe alone does the great Cæfar live;
    'Tis all the conquer'd world could give.
    We poets, madder yet than all,
With a refin'd fantaftic vanity,
Think, we not only have, but give eternity.
    Fain would I fee that prodigal,

and, by paffing through fo many hands, more inftru-
mental to the propagation of Cæfar's fame, than all the
glories of his life.

    [*b*] —*two immortal fyllables*] This lively ridicule, on
pofthumous fame, is well enough placed in a poem, or de-
clamation : but we are a little furprized to find fo grave
a writer, as Mr. Wollafton, diverting himfelf with it.
" In reality (fays he) the man is not known ever the more
" to pofterity, becaufe his name is tranfmitted to them :
" *he* doth not live, becaufe his *name* does. When it is
" faid, J. Cæfar fubdued Gaul, beat Pompey, changed
" the Roman commonwealth," &c.—*Rel. of Nat. Sect.*v.
—The fophiftry is apparent. Put *Cato* in the place of
Cæfar ; and then fee whether that great man do not
live in his name, *fubftantially*, that is, to good purpofe,
if the impreffion, which thofe *two immortal fyllables* make
on the mind, be of ufe in exciting pofterity, or any one
man, to the love and imitation of Cato's virtue.

                               Who

Who his to-morrow would beſtow
For all old Homer's life, e'er ſince he died, till now.

XVII.

On the Death of Mrs. CATHARINE PHILIPS [i].

CRUEL diſeaſe ! ah, could it not ſuffice
Thy old and conſtant ſpight to exerciſe
Againſt the gentleſt and the faireſt ſex,
Which ſtill thy depredations moſt do vex ?
Where ſtill thy malice moſt of all
(Thy malice or thy luſt) does on the faireſt fall ?
And in them moſt aſſault the faireſt place,
The throne of empreſs beauty, ev'n the face ?
There was enough of that here to aſſwage
(One would have thought) either thy luſt or rage;
Was't not enough, when thou, prophane diſeaſe,
Didſt on this glorious temple ſeize;

[i] This poem is preſerved, in honour of the lady,
here celebrated, who had the fortune to be equally
eſteemed by the beſt poet and beſt divine of her age.

Was't

Was't not enough, like a wild zealot, there,
All the rich outward ornaments to tear,
Deface the innocent pride of beauteous images ?
Was't not enough thus rudely to defile,
But thou muſt quite deſtroy, the goodly pile ?
And thy unbounded ſacrilege commit
On th' inward holieſt holy [*k*] of her wit ?
Cruel diſeaſe ! there thou miſtook'ſt thy power :
    No mine of death can that devour ;
On her embalmed name it will abide
    An everlaſting pyramide,
As high as heav'n the top, as earth the baſis wide.

2.

All ages paſt record, all countries now,
In various kinds, ſuch equal beauties ſhow,
    That ev'n judge Paris [*l*] would not know
On whom the golden apple to beſtow ;
Though goddeſſes to his ſentence did ſubmit,
Women and lovers would appeal from it :
Nor durſt he ſay, of all the female race,
    This is the ſovereign face.

[*k*] —*holieſt holy*] I wiſh the poet had forborn this alluſion.

[*l*] —*judge Paris*] Familiar, again, or rather bur-leſque; quite out of ſeaſon.

                And

And some (though these be of a kind that's rare,
That's much, ah, much less frequent, than the fair)
So equally renown'd for virtue are,
That it the mother of the gods might pose,
When the best woman for her guide she chose [m].
    But, if Apollo should design
    A woman laureat to make,
Without dispute he would Orinda take,
    Though Sappho and the famous Nine
      Stood by, and did repine.
      To be a princess or a queen,
Is great; but 'tis a greatness always seen;
The world did never but two women know,
Who, one by fraud, th' other by wit, did rise
To the two tops of spiritual dignities [n],
One female pope of old, one female poet now.

[m] Alluding to the introduction of the statue of *Cy-bele* into Rome: *Liv.* l. xxix. The goddess, indeed, had a long train of Roman matrons for her attendants. But, as the historian tells the story, she chose the *best man* in Rome for her *host*; not the *best woman*, for her *guide*. Whether the poet forgot himself, or purposely falsified the story for the sake of his application, I know not.

[n] —*spiritual dignities*] The English word, *spiritual*, as applied to dignities, means *religious* or *ecclesiastical*, in opposition to *civil* or *temporal*. But the French word *spirituel*, of like sound, means, also, *witty* or *intellectual*. Hence the *equivoque*; with which our poet was not a lit-

3. Of

3.

Of female poets, who had names of old,
   Nothing is ſhown, but only told ;
And all we hear of them perhaps may be
Male-flattery only, and male-poetry.
Few minutes did their beauties lightning waſte,
The thunder of their voice did longer laſt,
   But that, too, ſoon was paſt.
The certain proofs of our Orinda's wit,
In her own laſting characters are writ ;
And they will long my praiſe of them ſurvive,
   Though long perhaps, too, that may live.
The trade of glory manag'd by the pen,
Though great it be, and every where is found,
Does bring in but ſmall profit to us men ;
'Tis by the number of the ſharers drown'd.
Orinda, on the female coaſts of fame,
Ingroſſes all the goods of a poetic name :

tle pleaſed, as we may ſee by his repetition of it, in the
Complaint, St. ii.—
   " Among the *ſpiritual* lords of peaceful fame."
—He forgot, on this and other occaſions, his own de-
finition of true wit by negatives—
   " 'Tis not, when *two like words* make up *one noiſe.*"
               St. ii. 6.

    She

She does no partner with her fee;
Does all the bufinefs there alone, which we
Are forc'd to carry on by a whole company.

4.

But wit's like a luxuriant vine;
    Unlefs to virtue's prop it join,
  Firm and erect towards heaven bound:
Though it with beauteous leaves and pleafant fruit
    be crown'd,
It lies deform'd, and rotting on the ground.
    Now fhame and blufhes on us all,
    Who our own fex fuperior call!
Orinda does our boafting fex out-do,
Not in wit only, but in virtue too.
She does above our beft examples rife,
In hate of vice, and fcorn of vanities.
Never did fpirit of the manly make,
And dipt all o'er in learning's facred lake,
A temper more invulnerable take.
No violent paffion could an entrance find,
Into the tender goodnefs of her mind:
Through walls of ftone thofe furious bullets may
    Force their impetuous way;
When her foft breaft they hit, powerlefs and dead
    they lay.

                      5. The

5.

The fame of friendſhip [o], which ſo long had told
Of three or four illuſtrious names of old,
Till hoarſe and weary with the tale ſhe grew,
    Rejoices now t' have got a new,
    A new, and more ſurprizing ſtory,
Of fair Leucaſia's and Orinda's glory.
As when a prudent man does once perceive
That in ſome foreign country he muſt live,
The language and the manners he does ſtrive
    To underſtand and practice here,
    That he may come, no ſtranger there ;
So well Orinda did herſelf prepare,
In this much different clime, for her remove
To the glad world of poetry and love.

[o] *The fame of friendſhip*] Mrs. Philips was as much
famed for her *friendſhips,* as for her poetry. Dr. *J.
Taylor* addreſſed his diſcourſe *on the nature and offices of
friendſhip,* to this lady.

XVIII. HYMN.

XVIII.

H Y M N.

TO LIGHT [p].

FIRST-born of Chaos, who fo fair didft come
　　From the old Negro's darkfome womb!
　　Which when it faw the lovely child,
The melancholy mafs put on kind looks, and
　　fmil'd.

2.

Thou tide of glory, which no reft doft know,
　　But ever ebb, and ever flow!
　　Thou golden fhower of a true Jove!
Who does in thee defcend, and heaven to earth
　　make love!

[p] The moral ftrokes in this hymn amply atone for
the falfe wit and quaint imagery, in which it too much
abounds.—It was the malady of that age, to be only taken,
　　" With glitt'ring thoughts ftruck out at ev'ry line;"
　　　　　　　　　　　　　　　　　　　Pope.
And the abundance of Mr. Cowley's wit made it but
too eafy for him to regale the vitiated tafte of his
readers with this fort of entertainment.

　　　　　　　　　　　　　　　3. Hail,

3.

Hail, active nature's watchful life and health !
   Her joy, her ornament, and wealth !
   Hail to thy hufband, Heat, and thee !
Thou, the world's beauteous bride ! the lufty
      bridegroom, he !

4.

Say, from what golden quivers of the fky,
   Do all thy winged arrows fly ?
   Swiftnefs and Power by birth are thine :
From thy great fire they came ; thy fire, the
    Word Divine.

5.

'Tis, I believe, this archery to fhow,
   That fo much coft in colours thou
   And fkill in painting doft beftow
Upon thy ancient arms, the gawdy heavenly bow.

6.

Swift as light thoughts their empty carriere run,
   Thy race is finifh'd, when begun ;

Let a poft-angel ftart with thee [q],
And thou the goal of earth fhalt reach, as foon as he.

7.

Thou, in the moon's bright chariot proud and gay,
　　Doft thy bright wood of ftars furvey ;
　　And all the year doft with thee bring
Of thoufand flowery lights thine own noċturnal
　　fpring.

8.

Thou, Scythian-like, doft round thy lands above
　　The fun's gilt tent for ever move,
　　And ftill, as thou in pomp doft go,
'The fhining pageants of the world attend thy fhow.

9.

Nor, amidft all thefe triumphs, doft thou fcorn
　　The humble glow-worms to adorn,

[q] —poft-angel ftart with thee] One of the moft
glaring faults in the poetry of Mr. Cowley's age was the
debafing of great fentiments and images by low allufions
and vulgar expreffions. What the reader looked for, was
wit ; and he looked no farther : as if that rule of common fenfe had been a difcovery of yefterday—
　　" Expreffion is the drefs of thought, and ftill
　　" Appears more decent, as more fuitable."
　　　　　　　Pope, Effay on Crit. ver. 318.
　　　　　　　　　　　　　　　And

And with thofe living fpangles gild
(O greatnefs without pride!) the bufhes of the field.

10.

Night, and her ugly fubjects [r], thou doft fright,
 And Sleep, the lazy owl of night;
 Afham'd and fearful to appear.
They fkreen their horrid fhapes with the black
 hemifphere.

11.

With 'em there haftes, and wildly takes the alarm,
 Of painted dreams, a bufy fwarm;
 At the firft opening of thine eye,
The various clufters break, the antic atoms fly.

[r] *Night, and her ugly fubjects*, &c.]
 " Night and all her fickly dews,
 " Her fpectres wan," &c. ——
    Mr. Gray, in *The progrefs of poefy.*
This excellent writer, not unfrequently, alludes to paffages in Mr. Cowley, whofe manners and genius much
refembled his own. Both charm us with the *fpleen* of
virtue: and both were equally qualified, by the gifts of
nature, to adorn the nobler, and the more familiar
poetry.—The tafte, the execution, the fuccefs, were
happily on the fide of our late poet.
    O 2   12. The

12.

.The guilty ferpents, and obfcener beafts,
　　Creep confcious to their fecret refts :
　　Nature to thee does reverence pay,
Ill omens and ill fights removes out of thy way [*s*].

13.

At thy appearance, Grief itfelf is faid
　　To fhake his wings, and roufe his head ;
　　And cloudy Care has often took
A gentle beamy fmile reflected from thy look.

14.

At thy appearance, Fear itfelf grows bold ;
　　Thy fun-fhine melts away his cold.
　　Encourag'd at the fight of thee,
To the cheek colour comes, and firmnefs to the knee.

15.

Even Luft, the mafter of a harden'd face,
　　Blufhes, if thou beeft in the place ;

[*s*] *Ill omens and ill fights removes out of thy way.*]
Alluding to the old Roman fuperftition, which an-
xioufly provided, when a great general marched out of.
the city, that no inaufpicious object fhould obftruct or
pollute his paffage.

　　　　　　　　　　　　　　　　　　To

To Darknefs' curtains he retires,
In fympathizing night he rowls his fmoaky fires.

16.

When, goddefs, thou lift'ft up thy waken'd head
 Out of the morning's purple bed,
  Thy choir of birds about thee play,
And all the joyful world falutes the rifing day.

17.

The ghofts, and monfter fpirits, that did prefume
 A body's privilege to affume,
  Vanifh again invifibly,
And bodies gain again their vifibility.

18.

All the world's bravery, that delights our eyes,
 Is but thy feveral liveries :
  Thou the rich dye on them beftoweft ;
Thy nimble pencil paints this landfkip, as thou
   goeft.

19.

A crimfon garment in the rofe thou wear'ft ;
 A crown of ftudded gold thou bear'ft [*t*] ;

[*t*] *A crown of ftudded gold thou bear'ft*] In the
flower fo call'd, or *Crown Imperial.* The name of the
    O 3   The

The virgin lilies, in their white,
Are clad but with the lawn of almoſt naked light.

20.

The violet, ſpring's little infant, ſtands
    Girt in thy purple ſwadling-bands :
    On the fair tulip thou doſt doat ;
Thou cloath'ſt it in a gay and party-colour'd
    coat [*u*].

21.

With flame condens'd thou doſt the jewels fix,
    And ſolid colours in it mix :
    Flora herſelf envies, to ſee
Flowers fairer than her own, and durable as ſhe.

22.

Ah, goddeſs ! would thou could'ſt thy hand with-
    hold,
    And be leſs liberal to gold ;
    Did'ſt thou leſs value to it give,
Of how much care (alas) might'ſt thou poor man
    relieve !

flower, and of its *bearing*, being the ſame, he could not
well expreſs them *both*. Yet, in the connection which
this line has with the foregoing, the mention of *one* only,
has an ill effect.

    [*u*] Prettily alluding to Joſeph's *coat of many colours*,
Gen. xxxvii. 3, 4.

23. To

23.

To me, the fun [w] is more delightful far,
    And all fair days much fairer are.
    But few, ah wondrous few there be, ,
Who do not gold prefer, o goddefs, ev'n to thee.

24.

Through the foft ways of heaven, and air, and fea,
    Which open all their pores to thee ;
    Like a clear river, thou doft glide,
And with thy living ftream through the clofe chan-
    nels flide.

25.

But where firm bodies thy free courfe oppofe,
    Gently thy fource the land o'erflows ;
    Takes there poffeffion, and does make,
Of colours mingled, light, a thick and ftanding lake.

26.

But the vaft ocean of unbounded day
    In th' empyréan heaven does ftay.

[w] *To me the fun*] An inimitable ftanza, in which
the whole foul of the poet comes out, and fhines through
the pureft and cleareft expreffion : like one of the
virgin-lilies, he before celebrates,
    —" *clad with the lawn of almoft naked light.*"

Thy

Thy rivers, lakes, and springs below
From thence took firſt their riſe, thither at laſt muſt
   flow.

XIX.

To the ROYAL SOCIETY [*x*].

I.

PHILOSOPHY, the great and only heir
   Of all that human knowledge, which has been
Unforfeited by man's rebellious ſin,
   Though full of years he do appear,
(Philoſophy, I ſay, and call it, He,
For, whatſoe'er the painter's fancy be,
   It a male-virtue ſeems to me)
Has ſtill been kept in nonage till of late,
Nor manag'd or enjoy'd his vaſt eſtate :

[*x*] This poem (beſides its intrinſic merit) is entitled
to a place in this collection, from the relation it has to the
Propoſition for the advancement of experimental philoſophy ;
which the reader will find in the end of this volume. It
gives, too, an amiable picture of the poet's mind, in the
concluding panegyric on his friend, Dr. Sprat, who had
written the hiſtory of the *Royal Society*.

                                          Three

Three or four thousand years, one would have
     thought,
To ripeness and perfection might have brought
   A science so well bred and nurs'd [y],
And of such hopeful parts too at the first.
But, oh, the guardians and the tutors then,
(Some negligent, and some ambitious men)
   Would ne'er consent to set him free,
Or his own natural powers to let him see,
Lest that should put an end to their authority.

2.

That his own business he might quite forget,
They' amus'd him with the sports of wanton wit,
With the desserts of poetry they fed him [z],
Instead of solid meats t' increase his force;
Instead of vigorous exercise, they led him

[y] *A science so well bred and nurs'd*] By Pythagoras
and Democritus.

[z] *With the desserts of poetry they fed him*] Much of
the ancient philosophy, was only a luscious mythology.
The way of accounting for a natural phænomenon, was
to tell a pleasant story. I suppose, the author had especially in view Lord Bacon's *Sapientia veterum*, where
that wise man amused himself and others—*with the
sports of wanton wit.*

                      Into

Into the pleasant labyrinths of ever-fresh dis-
    course [*a*].
Instead of carrying him to see
The riches which do hoarded for him lie
    In nature's endless treasury,
    They chose his eye to entertain
    (His curious, but not covetous eye [*b*])
With painted scenes, and pageants of the brain [*c*].
Some few exalted spirits[*d*]this latter age has shown,
That labour'd to assert the liberty
(From guardians, who were now usurpers grown)
Of this old minor still, captiv'd philosophy;
    But 'twas rebellion call'd, to fight
    For such a long-oppressed right.

[*a*] *Into the pleasant labyrinths of ever-fresh discourse*]
The Platonic school, which joined *eloquence* to philosophy.

[*b*] *His* curious, *but not* covetous *eye*] i. e. ingenious
speculation, and not *use,* was the object of that philosophy.

[*c*] —*pageants of the brain*] The peripatetic fancies—
—"tricks to shew the stretch of human brain." Pope.

[*d*] *Some few exalted spirits*] P. Ramus, and his
followers, who *laboured to assert the liberty* of philosophy
from the usurped dominion of the Aristotelians; men,
who, under colour of *guarding* the rights of the old
philosophy, *tyrannized* over reason herself.

                            Bacon,

Bacon, at laft, a mighty man, arofe,
   Whom a wife king and nature chofe
   Lord chancellor of both their laws,
And boldly undertook the injur'd pupil's caufe.

3.

Authority, which did a body boaft,
Though 'twas but air condens'd and ftalk'd about,
Like fome old giant's more gigantic ghoft,
   To terrify the learned rout,
With the plain magic of true reafon's light,   .
   He chac'd out of our fight,
Nor fuffer'd living men to be mifled
   By the vain fhadows of the dead :
To graves, from whence it rofe, the conquer'd phan-
       tom fled ;
   [*f*]   *   *   *   *

4.

From words, which are but pictures of the thought,
 (Though we our thoughts from them perverfely drew)
To things, the mind's right object, he it brought :
Like foolifh birds, to painted grapes we flew ;
He fought, and gather'd for our ufe, the true ;

   [*f*] The reft of this ftanza is left out.

                       And,

   J

And, when on heaps the chosen bunches lay,
He press'd them wisely, the mechanic way [*f*],
Till all their juice did in one vessel join,
Ferment into a nourishment divine,
   The thirsty soul's refreshing wine.
Who to the life an exact piece would make,
Must not from others work a copy take [*g*];
   No, not from Rubens or Vandike;
Much less content himself to make it like
Th' ideas and the images, which lie
In his own fancy, or his memory [*h*].
  No, he before his sight must place
  The natural and living face [*i*];
   The real object must command
Each judgement of his eye, and motion of his hand.

[*f*] — *the mechanic way*] i. e. in the way of *experiment*.

[*g*] *Must not from others work a copy take*] As Gassendi did, whose philosophy is nothing more than a *copy*, a fine one indeed, from that of Epicurus. ANON.

[*h*] *Th' ideas and the images, which lie
In his own fancy, or his memory*] Meaning Des Cartes, who went to work in this manner, and spun a subtle cobweb theory out of his own brain. ANON.

[*i*] *The natural and living face*]
  " The naked nature and the living grace." Pope.

                  5. From

5.

From thefe, and all long errors of the way [k],
In which our wandering predeceffors went,
And, like th' old Hebrews, many years did ftray
　In defarts but of fmall extent,
Bacon, like Mofes, led us forth at laft;
　The barren wildernefs he paft,
　Did on the very border ftand
　Of the bleft promis'd land;
And, from the mountain's top of his exalted wit,
　Saw it himfelf, and fhew'd us it.
But life did never to one man allow
Time to difcover worlds, and conquer too;
Nor can fo fhort a line fufficient be
To fathom the vaft depths of nature's fea.
　The work he did, we ought t'admire,
And were unjuft, if we fhould more require
From his few years, divided 'twixt th' excefs
Of low affliction, and high happinefs [l].

[k] *—errors of the way*]   A beautiful Latinifm—
"*—pelagine* venis *erroribus* actus?" Virg. Æn. vi. 532.
"Sive *errore viæ*, feu tempeftatibus acti." Ib. vii. 199.
　[l]   *— 'twixt th' excefs*
Of low affliction and high happinefs]   So expreffed, as
to convey not only the poet's idea of this fituation,
but his *fenfe* of it.

　I   For

For who on things remote can fix his fight,
That's always in a triumph, or a fight ?

6.

From you, great champions, we expe&ct to get
Thefe fpacious countries, but difcover'd yet;
Countries, where yet, inftead of nature, we
Her images and idols worfhip'd fee :
Thefe large and wealthy regions to fubdue,
Though learning has whole armies at command,
   Quarter'd about in every land,
A better troop fhe ne'er together drew.
   Methinks, like Gideon's little band,
   God with defign has pick'd out you,
To do thefe noble wonders by a few :
When the whole hoft he faw, they are (faid he)
   Too many to o'ercome for me ;
   And now he chufes out his men,
   Much in the way, that he did then :
   Not thofe many, whom he found
   Idly extended on the ground,
   To drink with their deje&cted head
The ftream, juft fo as by their mouths it fled :
   No, but thofe few, who took the waters up,
And made of their laborious hands the cup.

7. Thus

7.

Thus you prepar'd ; and in the glorious fight
  Their wondrous pattern too [m] you'take :
'Their old and empty pitchers firft they brake,
And with their hands then lifted up the light.
  Io ! found too the trumpets here !
Already your victorious lights appear ;
New fcenes of heaven already we efpy,
And crowds of golden worlds on high ;
Which, from the fpacious plains of earth and fea,
  Could never yet difcover'd be
By failors or Chaldæans watchful eye.
Nature's great works no diftance can obfcure ;
No fmallnefs her near objects can fecure ;
  Ye have taught the curious fight to prefs
  Into the privateft recefs
Of her imperceptible littlenefs.
  Ye have learn'd to read her fmalleft hand,
And well begun her deepeft fenfe to underftand.

8.

Mifchief and true difhonour fall on thofe,
Who would to laughter or to fcorn [n] expofe

[m] *Their wondrous pattern too*] His lavifh wit never
knows when to have done with an allufion.
  [n] *—to laughter or to fcorn*] It is not to be conceived

So virtuous and fo noble a defign,
So human for its ufe, for knowledge fo divine.
The things, which thefe proud men defpife, and call
  Impertinent and vain, and fmall,
Thofe fmalleft things of nature let me know,
Rather than all their greateft actions do.
Whoever would depofed truth advance
  Into the throne ufurp'd from it,
Muft feel at firft the blows of ignorance,
  And the fharp points of envious wit.
So when, by various turns of the celeftial dance,
  In many thoufand years
  A ftar, fo long unknown appears,
Though heaven itfelf more beauteous by it grow,
It troubles and alarms the world below,
Does to the wife a ftar, to fools a meteor, fhow.

9.

With courage and fuccefs you the bold work begin;
  Your cradle has not idle been :

what ridicule this fociety drew upon itfelf from the wits
on its firft inftitution —
    "But fenfe furviv'd, when merry jefts were paft;
    "For rifing merit will buoy up at laft."   Pope.
                                          None.

None e'er but Hercules and you, could be
At five years age worthy a hiftory.
   And ne'er did fortune better yet
   Th' hiftorian [o] to the ftory fit:
As you from all old errors free
And purge the body of philofophy;
   So from all modern follies he
Has vindicated eloquence and wit.
His candid ftyle, like a clean ftream, does flide,
   And his bright fancy all the way
   Does like the fun-fhine in it play;
It does, like Thames, the beft of rivers, glide,
Where the god does not rudely overturn,
   But gently pour, the cryftal urn,
And with judicious hand does the whole current
    guide.
'T has all the beauties, nature can impart,
And all the comely drefs, without the paint of art.

[o] Dr. Sprat.

XX.

THE COMPLAINT [*p*].

I.

IN a deep vision's intellectual scene,
  Beneath a bower for sorrow made
    Th' uncomfortable shade,
  Of the black yew's unlucky green,
Mix'd with the mourning willow's careful grey,
Where reverend Cam cuts out his famous way,
    The melancholy Cowley lay :
And lo! a Muse appear'd to his clos'd sight,
(The Muses oft in lands of vision play)
Bodied, array'd, and seen by an internal light.

[*p*] The plan of this poem is highly poetical : and,
though the numbers be not the most pleasing, the expression is almost every where natural and beautiful.
But its principal charm is that air of melancholy, thrown
over the whole, so expressive of the poet's character.

The *address* of the writer is seen in conveying his just
reproaches on the *court*, under a pretended vindication
of it against the *Muse*.

A gol-

A golden harp, with filver ftrings, fhe bore;
A wondrous hieroglyphic robe fhe wore,
In which all colours and all figures were,
That nature or that fancy can create,
 That art can never imitate;
And with loofe pride it wanton'd in the air.
In fuch a drefs, in fuch a well-cloath'd dream,
She us'd, of old, near fair Ifmenus' ftream,
Pindar her Theban favourite to meet;
A crown was on her head, and wings were on her
  feet.

2.

She touch'd him with her harp, and rais'd him
  from the ground;
The fhaken ftrings melodioufly refound:
 Art thou return'd at laft, faid fhe,
 To this forfaken place and me?
Thou prodigal, who didft fo loofely wafte
Of all thy youthful years, the good eftate;
Art thou return'd here, to repent too late?
And gather hufks of learning up at laft,
Now the rich harveft-time of life is paft,
 And winter marches on fo faft?
But, when I meant t' adopt thee for my fon,
And did as learn'd a portion affign,
As ever any of the mighty Nine
 Had to their deareft children done;

When

When I refolv'd t' exalt thy' anointed name,
Among the fpiritual lords [q] of peaceful fame;
Thou changeling, thou, bewitch'd with noife and
     fhow,
Wouldft into courts and cities from me go;
Wouldft fee the world abroad, and have a fharc
In all the follies and the tumults there,
Thou wouldft, forfooth, be fomething in a ftate,
And bufinefs thou wouldft find, and wouldft create:
    Bufinefs! the frivolous pretence
Of human lufts, to fhake off innocence;
    Bufinefs! the grave impertinence:
Bufinefs! the thing which I of all things hate,
Bufinefs! the contradiction of thy fate.

3.

Go, renegado, caft up thy account,
    And fee to what amount
    Thy foolifh gains by quitting me:
The fale of knowledge, fame, and liberty,
The fruits of thy unlearn'd apoftacy.

[q] —*Spiritual Lords*] Alluding to the ftyle of the
Houfe of Lords—*the Lords Spiritual and Temporal.*—But
fee the note on *fpiritual dignities,* p. 188.

Thou

Thou thought'ft, if once the public ftorm were paft,
All thy remaining life fhould fun-fhine be :
Behold, the public ftorm is fpent at laft,
The fovereign is toft at fea no more,
And thou, with all the noble company,
     Art got at laft to fhore.
But, whilft thy fellow-voyagers I fee
All march'd up to poffefs the promis'd land,
Thou ftill alone (alas) doft gaping ftand,
Upon the naked beach, upon the barren fand.

4.

As a fair morning of the bleffed fpring,
    After a tedious ftormy night;
Such was the glorious entry of our king,
Enriching moifture drop'd on every thing :
Plenty he fow'd below, and caft about him light.
    But then (alas) to thee alone,
One of old Gideon's miracles was fhown :
For every tree, and every herb around,
    With pearly dew was crown'd,
    And upon all the quicken'd ground,
The fruitful feed of heaven did brooding lie;
And nothing but the Mufe's fleece was dry.
    It did all other threats furpafs,
When God to his own people faid,

(The

(The men, whom through long wanderings he
  had led).
  That he would give them ev'n a heaven of brafs:
They look'd up to that heaven in vain,
That bounteous heaven, which God did not reftrain,
Upon the moft unjuft to fhine and rain.

5.

The Rachel [r], for which twice feven years and
  more,
  Thou didft with faith and labour ferve,
And didft (if faith and labour can) deferve,
  Though fhe contracted was to thee,
  Giv'n to another thou didft fee;
  Giv'n to another, who had ftore
Of fairer, and of richer wives, before;
And not a Leah left, thy recompence to be,
Go on, twice feven years more, thy fortune try;
Twice feven years more, God in his bounty may
  Give thee, to fling away
Into the court's deceitful lottery,
  But think how likely 'tis, that thou,
With the dull work of thy unweildy plough,

[r] *The Rachel*] The mafterfhip of the Savoy.

         Shouldft

Shouldſt in a hard and barren ſeaſon thrive,
   Shouldſt even able be to live ;
Thou, to whoſe ſhare ſo little bread did fall,
In the miraculous year, when manna rain'd on all.

6.

Thus ſpake the Muſe, and ſpake it with a ſmile,
That ſeem'd at once to pity and revile.
And to her thus, raiſing his thoughtful head,
   The melancholy Cowley ſaid ;
   Ah wanton foe, doſt thou upbraid
   The ills, which thou thyſelf haſt made ?
When, in the cradle, innocent I lay,
Thou, wicked ſpirit, ſtoleſt me away,
   And my abuſed ſoul didſt bear
Into thy new-found worlds, I know not where,
   Thy golden Indies in the air :
   And ever ſince I ſtrive in vain
   My raviſh'd freedom to regain ;
   Still I rebel, ſtill thou doſt reign ;
Lo, ſtill in verſe againſt thee I complain.
   There is a ſort of ſtubborn weeds,
Which, if the earth but once it ever breeds,
   No wholeſome herb can near them thrive,
   No uſeful plant can keep alive :
         The

The foolish sports I did on thee bestow,
Make all my art and labour fruitless now ;
Where once such Fairies dance, no grass [*s*] doth
    ever grow.

7.

When my new mind had no infusion known,
Thou gav'st so deep a tincture of thine own,
    That ever since I vainly try
    To wash away th' inherent dye :
Long work perhaps may spoil thy colours quite,
But never will reduce the native white :
    To all the ports of honour and of gain
    I often steer my course in vain ;
Thy gale comes crofs, and drives me back again.
Thou slack'nest all my nerves of industry,
    By making them so oft to be
The tinkling strings of thy loose minstrelsy.

[*s*] — *no grass*] i. e, no grass which turns to profit.——
The poet alludes, in this verse, to the *four ringlets*,
which are sometimes found in pasture-grounds, and, according to the philosophy of the country-people, are oc-
casioned by fairies dancing upon them. He had pro-
bably his eye on that fine passage of Shakespear,

        —— " ye demy-puppets, that
  " By moon-shine do the green four ringlets make,
  " Whereof the ewe not bites"——
                Tempest, Act v. S. ii.
                  Whoever

Whoever this world's happinefs would fee,
  Muft as entirely caft off thee,
  As they, who only heaven defire,
  Do from the world retire.
This was my error, this my grofs miftake,
Myfelf a demy-votary to make.
Thus, with Sapphira and her hufband's fate,
(A fault which I, like them, am taught too late)
For all that I give up, I nothing gain,
And perifh for the part which I retain.

8.

Teach me not, then, o thou fallacious Mufe,
    The court, and better king [*t*], t' accufe ;
The heaven, under which I live, is fair ;
The fertile foil will a full harveft bear ;
Thine, thine, is all the barrennefs ; if thou
Mak'ft me fit ftill and fing, when I fhould plough :

[*t*] —*better king*] i. e. *better* in his own nature, than
the court [his minifters] would allow him to be. The
fuppofition was decent, but not true. The minifter of
that time was juft, nay generous, to our poet. [See *Lord
Clarendon's Life*, Part i. 16.] But, unluckily, the poet's
patrons were the minifter's moft determined enemies.
In the mean time, *the better king* cared neither for the
minifter, nor the poet.

                                        When

When I but think, how many a tedious year
    Our patient sovereign did attend
    His long misfortunes' fatal end !
How chearfully, and how exempt from fear,
On the great Sovereign's will he did depend ;
I ought to be accurs'd, if I refuse
To wait on his, o thou fallacious Muse!
Kings have long hands (they say) ; and though I be
So distant, they may reach at length to me.
    However, of all princes, thou
Should'st not reproach rewards, for being small
        or slow ;
Thou, who rewardest but with popular breath,
    And that too, after death.

END OF THE POEMS.

ΠΛΕΟΝ ΗΜΙΣΥ ΠΑΝΤΟΣ.

A PRO-

A

PROPOSITION

FOR

The ADVANCEMENT of EXPERI-
MENTAL PHILOSOPHY [*a*].

THE COLLEGE.

THAT the philofophical college be
fituated within one, two, or (at far-
theft) three miles of London ; and, if it

[*a*] Ingenious men delight in dreams of reformation.—In comparing this *Propofition* of Cowley, with
that of Milton, addreffed to Mr. Hartlib, we find that
thefe great poets had amufed themfelves with fome
exalted, and, in the main, congenial fancies, on the
fubject of education : that, of the *two* plans, propofed,
this of Mr. Cowley was better digefted, and is the *lefs*
fanciful ; if a preference, in this refpect, can be given
to either, when both are manifeftly Utopian : and that
our univerfities, in their prefent form, are well enough
calculated to anfwer all the reafonable ends of fuch
inftitutions ; provided we allow for the unavoidable
defects of them, when drawn out into practice.

be

be poffible to find that convenience, upon the fide of the river, or very near it.

That the revenue of this college amount to four thoufand pounds a year.

That the company received into it be as follows :

1. Twenty philofophers or profeffors. 2. Sixteen young fcholars, fervants to the profeffors. 3. A chaplain. 4. A bailiff for the revenue. 5. A manciple or purveyor for the provifions of the houfe. 6. Two gardeners. 7. A mafter-cook. 8. An under-cook. 9. A butler. 10. An under-butler. 11. A furgeon. 12. Two lungs, or chemical fervants. 13. A library-keeper, who is likewife to be apothecary, druggift, and keeper of inftruments, engines, &c. 14. An officer, to feed and take care of all beafts, fowl, &c. kept by the college. 15. A groom of the ftable. 16. A meffenger, to fend up and down for all ufes of the college. 17. Four old women, to tend the chambers, keep the houfe clean, and fuch like fervices.

That

That the annual allowance for this company be as follows : 1. To every profeſſor, and to the chaplain, one hundred and twenty pounds. 2. To the ſixteen ſcholars twenty pounds apiece, ten pounds for their diet, and ten pounds for their entertainment. 3. To the bailiff, thirty pounds, beſides allowance for his journies. 4. To the purveyor, or manciple, thirty pounds. 5. To each of the gardeners, twenty pounds. 6. To the maſter-cook, twenty pounds. 7. To the under-cook, four pounds. 8. To the butler, ten pounds. 9. To the under-butler, four pounds. 10. To the ſurgeon, thirty pounds. 11. To the library-keeper, thirty pounds. 12. To each of the lungs, twelve pounds. 13. To the keeper of the beaſts, ſix pounds. 14. To the groom, five pounds. 15. To the meſſenger, twelve pounds. 16. To the four neceſſary women, ten pounds. For the manciples table, at which all the ſervants of the houſe are to eat, except the ſcholars, one hundred and ſixty pounds. For three

horſes

horfes for the fervice of the college, thirty pounds.

All which amounts to three thoufand two hundred eighty-five pounds. So that there remains, for keeping of the houfe and gardens, and operatories, and inftruments, and animals, and experiments of all forts, and all other expences, feven hundred and fifteen pounds.

Which were a very inconfiderable fum for the great ufes to which it is defigned, but that I conceive the induftry of the college will in a fhort time fo enrich itfelf, as to get a far better ftock for the advance and enlargement of the work when it is once begun: neither is the continuance of particular mens liberality to be defpaired of, when it fhall be encouraged by the fight of that public benefit which will accrue to all mankind, and chiefly to our nation, by this foundation. Something likewife will arife from leafes and other cafualties; that nothing of which may be diverted to the private gain of the profeffors, or any other

ufe

I

ufe befides that of the fearch of nature, and
by it the general good of the world, and
that care may be taken for the certain per-
formance of all things ordained by the
inftitution, as likewife for the protection
and encouragement of the company, it is
propofed :

That fome perfon of eminent quality, a
lover of folid learning, and no ftranger in
it; be chofen chancellor or prefident of the
college ; and that eight governors more,
men qualified in the like manner, be joined with him, two of which fhall yearly be
appointed vifitors of the college, and receive an exact account of all expences even
to the fmalleft, and of the true eftate of their
public treafure, under the hands and oaths
of the profeffors refident.

That the choice of profeffors in any vacancy belong to the chancellor and the governors; but that the profeffors (who are likeli-
eft to know what men of the nation are moft
proper for the duties of their fociety) direct
their choice, by recommending two or three
perfons

perſons to them at every election : and
that, if any learned perſon within his majeſty's dominions diſcover, or eminently improve, any uſeful kind of knowledge, he
may upon that ground, for his reward and
the encouragement of others, be preferred,
if he pretend to the place, before any body
elſe.

That the governors have power to turn
out any profeſſor, who ſhall be proved to
be either ſcandalous or unprofitable to
the ſociety.

That the college be built after this, or
ſome ſuch manner : That it conſiſt of three
fair quadrangular courts, and three large
grounds, incloſed with good walls behind
them. That the firſt court be built with
a fair cloiſter ; and the profeſſors lodgings,
or rather little houſes, four on each ſide, at
ſome diſtance from one another, and with
little gardens behind them, juſt after the
manner of the Chartreux beyond ſea. That
the inſide of the cloiſter be lined with a
gravel-walk, and that walk with a row of
trees ;

trees; and that in the middle there be a parterre of flowers and a fountain.

That the second quadrangle, juſt behind the firſt, be ſo contrived, as to contain theſe parts. · 1. A chapel. 2. A hall, with two long tables on each ſide, for the ſcholars and officers of the houſe to eat at, and with a pulpit and forms at the end for the public lectures. 3. A large and pleaſant dining-room within the hall, for the profeſſors to eat in, and to hold their aſſemblies and conferences. 4. A public ſchool-houſe. 5. A library. 6. A gallery to walk in, adorned with the pictures or ſtatues of all the inventors of any thing uſeful to human life; as printing, guns, America, &c. and of late in anatomy, the circulation of the blood, the milky veins, and ſuch like diſcoveries in any art, with ſhort elogies under the portraitures: as likewiſe the figures of all ſorts of creatures, and the ſtuft ſkins of as many ſtrange animals as can be gotten. 7. An anatomy-chamber, adorned with ſkeletons and anatomical pictures, and prepared with all conveniences for diffection. 8. A chamber for all manner of drugs, and apothecaries materials. 9. A mathematical chamber, furnished with all forts of mathematical inftruments, being an appendix to the library. 10. Lodgings for the chaplain, furgeon, library-keeper, and purveyor, near the chapel, anatomy-chamber, library, and hall.

That the third court be on one fide of thefe, very large, but meanly built, being defigned only for ufe, and not for beauty too as the others. That it contain the kitchen, butteries, brew-houfe, bake-houfe, dairy, lardry, ftables, &c. and efpecially great laboratories for chemical operations, and lodgings for the under-fervants.

That behind the fecond court be placed the garden, containing all forts of plants that our foil will bear; and at the end a little houfe of pleafure, a lodge for the gardener, and a grove of trees cut out into walks.

That the fecond inclofed ground be a garden, deftined only to the trial of all

manner

manner of experiments concerning plants, as their melioration, acceleration, retardation, conservation, composition, transmutation, coloration, or whatsoever else can be produced by art either for use or curiosity, with a lodge in it for the gardener.

That the third ground be employed in convenient receptacles for all sorts of creatures which the professors shall judge necessary, for their more exact search into the nature of animals, and the improvement of their uses to us.

That there be likewise built, in some place of the college where it may serve most for ornament of the whole, a very high tower for observation of celestial bodies, adorned with all sorts of dials and such like curiosities; and that there be very deep vaults made under ground, for experiments most proper to such places, which will be undoubtedly very many.

Much might be added; but truly I am afraid this is too much already for the charity or generosity of this age to extend to; and we do not defign this after the model of Solomon's houfe in my Lord Bacon (which is a projeϵt for experiments that can never be experimented), but propofe it within fuch bounds of expence as have often been exceeded by the buildings of private citizens.

OF THE PROFESSORS, SCHOLARS, CHAPLAIN, AND OTHER OFFICERS.

THAT of the twenty profeffors four be always travelling beyond feas, and fixteen always refident, unlefs by permiffion upon extraordinary occafions; and every one fo abfent, leaving a deputy behind him to fupply his duties.

That the four profeffors itinerant be affigned to the four parts of the world, Europe, Afia, Africa, and America, there to refide three years at leaft; and to give a conftant account of all things that belong to the learning, and efpecially natural experimental philofophy, of thofe parts.

That

That the expence of all difpatches, and all books, fimples, animals, ftones, metals, minerals, &c. and all curiofities whatfoever, natural or artificial, fent by them to the college, fhall be defrayed out of the trea-fury, and an additional allowance (above the 120 *l.*) made to them as foon as the college's revenue fhall be improved.

That, at their going abroad, they fhall take a folemn oath, never to write any thing to the college, but what, after very diligent examination, they fhall fully believe to be true, and to confefs and recant it as foon as they find themfelves in an error.

That the fixteen profeffors refident fhall be bound to ftudy and teach all forts of natural, experimental philofophy, to con-fift of the mathematics, mechanics, medi-cine, anatomy, chemiftry, the hiftory of animals, plants, minerals, elements, &c. ; agriculture, architecture, art military, na-vigation, gardening ; the myfteries of all trades, and improvement of them ; the facture of all merchandizes, all natural ma-

gic

gic or divination; and briefly all things contained in the catalogue of natural histories annexed to my Lord Bacon's Organon.

That once a day from Easter till Michaelmas, and twice a week from Michaelmas to Easter, at the hours in the afternoon most convenient for auditors from London, according to the time of the year, there shall be a lecture read in the hall, upon such parts of natural experimental philosophy, as the professors shall agree on among themselves, and as each of them shall be able to perform usefully and honourably.

That two of the professors, by daily, weekly, or monthly turns, shall teach the public schools, according to the rules hereafter prescribed.

That all the professors shall be equal in all respects (except precedency, choice of lodging, and such like privileges, which shall belong to seniority in the college); and that all shall be masters and treasurers by annual turns, which two officers for the time

time being fhall take place of all the reft, and fhall be *arbitri duarum menfarum.*

That the mafter fhall command all the officers of the college, appoint affemblies or conferences upon occafion, and prefide in them with a double voice; and in his abfence the treafurer, whofe bufinefs is to receive and difburfe all monies by the maf-ter's order in writing (if it be an extraor-dinary), after confent of the other pro-feffors.

That all the profeffors fhall fup together in the parlour within the hall every night, and fhall dine there twice a week (to wit, Sundays and Thurfdays) at two round ta-bles, for the convenience of difcourfe, which fhall be for the moft part of fuch matters as may improve their ftudies and profef-fions; and to keep them from falling into loofe or unprofitable talk, fhall be the duty of the two *arbitri menfarum,* who may like-wife command any of the fervant-fcholars to read to them what he fhall think fit, whilft they are at table: that it fhall belong

Q 4 like-

likewife to the faid *arbitri menfarum* only, to invite ftrangers; which they fhall rarely do, unlefs they be men of learning or great parts, and fhall not invite above two at a time to one table, nothing being more vain and unfruitful than numerous meetings of aequaintance.

That the profeffors refident fhall allow the college twenty pounds a year for their diet, whether they continue there all the time or not.

That they fhall have once a week an affembly, or conference, concerning the affairs of the college and the progrefs of their experimental philofophy.

That, if any one find out any thing which he conceives to be of confequence, he fhall communicate it to the affembly, to be examined, experimented, approved, or rejected.

That, if any one be author of an invention that may bring in profit, the third part of it fhall belong to the inventor, and the two other to the fociety; and befides if the

thing

thing be very confiderable, his ftatue or picture, with an elogy under it fhall be placed in the gallery, and made a denifon of that corporation of famous men.

That all the profeffors fhall be always affigned to fome particular inquifition (befides the ordinary courfe of their ftudies), of which they fhall give an account to the affembly; fo that by this means there may be every day fome operation or other made in all the arts, as chemiftry, anatomy, mechanics, and the like; and that the college fhall furnifh for the charge of the operation.

That there fhall be kept a regifter under lock and key, and not to be feen but by the profeffors, of all the experiments that fucceed, figned by the perfons who made the trial.

That the popular and received errors in experimental philofophy (with which, like weeds in a neglected garden, it is now almoft all over-grown) fhall be evinced by trial, and taken notice of in the public
lectures,

lectures, that they may no longer abuse the credulous, and beget new ones by confequence or fimilitude.

That every third year (after the full fettlement of the foundation) the college fhall give an account in print, in proper and antient Latin, of the fruits of their triennial induftry.

That every profeffor refident fhall have his fcholar to wait upon him in his chamber and at table; whom he fhall be obliged to breed up in natural philofophy, and render an account of his progrefs to the affembly, from whofe election he received him, and therefore is refponfible to it, both for the care of his education and the juft and civil ufage of him.

That the fcholar fhall underftand Latin very well, and be moderately initiated in the Greek, before he be capable of being chofen into the fervice; and that he fhall not remain in it above feven years.

That his lodging fhall be with the profeffor whom he ferves.

That

That no profeffor fhall be a married man, or a divine, or lawyer in practice; only phyfic he may be allowed to prefcribe, becaufe the ftudy of that art is a great part of the duty of his place, and the duty of that is fo great, that it will not fuffer him to lofe much time in mercenary practice.

That the profeffors fhall, in the college, wear the habit of ordinary mafters of art in the univerfities, or of doctors, if any of them be fo.

That they fhall all keep an inviolable and exemplary friendfhip with one another; and that the affembly fhall lay a confidera-ble pecuniary mulct upon any one who fhall be proved to have entered fo far into a quarrel as to give uncivil language to his brother-profeffor; and that the per-feverance in any enmity fhall be punifhed by the governors with expulfion.

That the chaplain fhall eat at the mafter's table (paying his twenty pounds a year as the others do); and that he fhall read prayers once a day at leaft, a little before fupper-time;

time ; that he ſhall preach in the chapel every Sunday morning, and catechize in the afternoon the ſcholars and the ſchool-boys ; that he ſhall every month adminiſter the holy ſacrament ; that he ſhall not trouble himſelf and his auditors with the contro-verſies of divinity, but only teach God in his juſt commandments, and in his won-derful works.

THE SCHOOL.

THAT the ſchool may be built ſo as to contain about two hundred boys.

That it be divided into four claſſes, not as others are ordinarily into ſix or ſeven; becauſe we ſuppoſe that the children ſent hither, to be initiated in things as well as words, ought to have paſt the two or three firſt, and to have attained the age of about thirteen years, being already well advanced in the Latin grammar, and ſome authors.

That none, though never ſo rich, ſhall pay any thing for their teaching ; and that, if any profeſſor ſhall be convicted to have

taken

taken any money in confideration of his pains in the fchool, he fhall be expelled with ignominy by the governors; but if any perfons of great eftate and quality, finding their fons much better proficients in learning here, ιthan boys of the fame age commonly are at other fchools, fhall not think fit to receive an obligation of fo near concernment without returning fome marks of acknowledgment, they may, if they pleafe, (for nothing is to be demanded) beftow fome little rarity or curiofity upon the fociety, in recompence of their trouble. ·

And becaufe it is deplorable to confider the lofs which children make of their time at moft fchools, employing, or rather cafting away, fix or feven years in the learning of words only, and that too very imperfectly :

That a method be here eftablifhed, for the infufing knowledge and language at the fame time into them ; and that this may be their apprenticefhip in natural philofophy. This, we conceive, may be done,

by

by breeding them up in authors, or pieces
of authors, who treat of some parts of nature, and who may be understood with as
much ease and pleasure, as those which are
commonly taught; such are, in Latin,
Varro, Cato, Columella, Pliny, part of
Celsus and of Seneca, Cicero de Divina-
tione, de Naturâ Deorum, and several scattered pieces, Virgil's Georgics, Grotius,
Nemesianus, Manilius : And because the
truth is, we want good poets (I mean we
have but few), who have purposely treated
of solid and learned, that is, natural matters (the most part indulging to the weak-
ness of the world, and feeding it either with
the follies of love, or with the fables of gods
and heroes), we conceive that one book
ought to be compiled of all the scattered
little parcels among the antient poets that
might serve for the advancement of natural
science, and which would make no small
or unuseful or unpleasant volume. To
this we would have added the morals and
rhetorics of Cicero, and the institutions of ·

Quincti-

Quinctilian; and for the comedians, from whom almoft all that neceffary part of common difcourfe, and all the moft intimate proprieties of-the language are drawn, we conceive, the boys may be made mafters of them, as a part of their recreation, and not of their tafk, if once a month, or at leaft once in two, they act one of Terence's Comedies, and afterwards (the moft advanced) fome of Plautus's; and this is for many reafons one of the beft exercifes they can be enjoined, and moft innocent pleafures they can be allowed. As for the Greek authors, they may ftudy Nicander, Oppianus (whom Scaliger does not doubt to prefer above Homer himfelf, and place next to his adored Virgil), Ariftotle's hiftory of animals, and other parts, Theophraftus and Diofcorides of plants, and a collection made out of feveral both poets and other Grecian writers. For the morals and rhetoric, Ariftotle may fuffice, or Hermogenes and Longinus be added for the latter. With the hiftory of animals they fhould

be

be shewed anatomy as a divertisement, and made to know the figures and natures of those creatures which are not common among us, disabusing them at the same time of those errors which are universally admitted concerning many. The same method should be used to make them acquainted with all plants ; and to this must be added a little of the antient and modern geography, the understanding of the globes, and the principles of geometry and astronomy. They should likewise use to declaim in Latin and English, as the Romans did in Greek and Latin; and in all this travel be rather led on by familiarity, encouragement, and emulation, than driven by severity, punishment, and terror. Upon festivals and play-times, they should exercise themselves in the fields, by riding, leaping, fencing, mustering and training after the manner of soldiers, &c. And, to prevent all dangers and all disorder, there should always be two of the scholars with them, to be as witnesses and directors of their actions ; in foul weather, it would

not

not be amifs for them to learn to dance, that is, to learn juft fo much (for all beyond is fuperfluous, if not worfe) as may give them a graceful comportment of their bodies.

Upon Sundays, and all days of devotion, they are to be a part of the chaplain's province.

That, for all thefe ends, the college fo order it, as that there may be fome convenient and pleafant houfes thereabouts, kept by religious, difcreet, and careful perfons, for the lodging and boarding of young fcholars; that they have a conftant eye over them, to fee that they be bred up there pioufly, cleanly, and plentifully, according to the proportion of the parents expences.

And that the college, when it fhall pleafe God, either by their own induftry and fuccefs, or by the benevolence of patrons, to enrich them fo far, as that it may come to their turn, and duty to be charitable to others, fhall, at their own charges, erect and maintain fome houfe or houfes for the entertainment of fuch poor mens fons, whofe good natural parts may promife either ufe or ornament to the commonwealth, during the time of their abode at fchool ; and fhall take care that it fhall be done with the fame conveniences as are enjoyed even by rich mens children (though they maintain the fewer for that caufe), there being nothing of eminent and illuftrious to be expected from a low, fordid, and hofpital-like education.

CONCLUSION.

IF I be not much abufed by a natural fondnefs to my own conceptions (that copyn of the Greeks, which no other language has a proper word for), there was never any project thought upon, which deferves to meet with fo few adverfaries as this ; for who can without impudent folly oppofe the eftablifhment of twenty wellfelected perfons in fuch a condition of life, that their whole bufinefs and fole profeffion may be to ftndy the improvement

and

and advantage of all other profeffions, from
that of the higheft general even to the low-
eft artifan ? who fhall be obliged to employ their whole time, wit, learning, and
induftry, to thefe four, the moft ufeful
that can be imagined, and to no other
ends ; firft, to weigh, examine, and prove
all things of nature delivered to us by
former ages ; to detect, explode, and ftrike
a cenfure through all falfe monies with
which the world has been paid and cheated
fo long ; and (as I may fay) to fet the mark
of the college upon all true coins, that they
may pafs hereafter without any farther trial :
fecondly, to recover the loft inventions,
and, as it were, drowned lands of the ancients : thirdly, to improve all arts which
we now have ; and laftly, to difcover others
which we yet have not : and who fhall
befides all this (as a benefit by the bye),
give the beft education in the world (purely
gratis) to as many mens children as fhall
think fit to make ufe of the obligation ?
Neither does it at all check or interfere with
any

any parties in a ſtate or religion; but is indifferently to be embraced by all differences in opinion, and can hardly be conceived capable (as many good inſtitutions have done) even of degeneration into any thing harmful. So that, all things conſidered, I will ſuppoſe this propoſition ſhall encounter with no enemies: the only queſtion is, whether it will find friends enough to carry it on from diſcourſe and deſign to reality and effect; the neceſſary expences of the beginning (for it will maintain itſelf well enough afterwards) being ſo great (though I have ſet them as low as is poſſible in order to ſo vaſt a work), that it may ſeem hopeleſs to raiſe ſuch a ſum out of thoſe few dead relics of human charity and public generoſity which are yet remaining in the world.

THE END OF VOL. I.

www.ingramcontent.com/pod-product-compliance
Lightning Source LLC
Chambersburg PA
CBHW031423020726
47499CB00005B/1571